W9-BGE-908

THE TRUTH ABOUT GOLF AND OTHER LIES

by

Buddy Hackett

Drawings by Gahan Wilson

DOUBLEDAY AND COMPANY, INC.
GARDEN CITY, NEW YORK

Copyright © 1968 by Buddy Hackett, Benjamin Yanow
and Paul J. Sherman, as Trustees

Library of Congress Catalog Card No. 68-29284
Manufactured in the United States of America

PUBLISHING CONSULTANT: J. P. Tarcher, Inc.

SECOND PRINTING

I dedicate this book to Mrs. Frank Faske

who gave her husband a set of golf sticks

which he couldn't or wouldn't use and which

he gave to me,

and

to 1957 when I hit a good shot and

to 1963 when I did it again.

They were two wonderful years.

"Golf is more fun than walking naked in a strange place, but not much."

B. Hackett

Contents

Most of my thoughts about golf involve the wonderful days I had in a foursome with Phil Foster, Joey Bishop, and Dick Shawn. We played almost every day in any kind of weather and without being disturbed or bothered by a thing called show business. In fact, when we would come back off the road and see each other again, our only thoughts were, "Who did you play with? Where did you play? How did you score?" No one ever cared very much about how many people did you draw? Was it a good room to work in? How is the sound system? What was the boss like? These things weren't important. The important thing was the game.

In those days I was free as the proverbial bird. I was unmarried. I had made no big inroads into show business, I was carefree and happy and didn't care about anything except a laugh, a laugh with the peculiar twist that cannot readily be duplicated.

Like one afternoon I was playing at the Concord International Golf Course in a foursome with Jimmy Demaret, Jan Murray, and somebody else whose name must be legion, because to this day I have met 1,163 people who claimed that they were the fourth and have told me, "Remember what you did . . ." And this is what I did.

At the 12th tee, Jan hit a beautiful drive, just the right amount to the left side of the fairway. A drive like that was quite unusual for him. In fact, to this day we all refer to it as the time Jan got a drive off. Then the somebody else in the foursome — who could have been any one of 1,163 people, hit a beautiful drive. Demaret's drive, of course, was magnificent. I, however, sliced it into the woods on the right side and went into the trees after it.

Picture this — a beautiful morning in late summer, the birds

twittering, crickets rubbing their knees together, and all manner of strange phenomenon going on. I wondered why my feet weren't cloven hooves as I felt like Pan, the boy god. Suddenly I was hampered by my clothing and started to disrobe, and soon I was naked as a jaybird, except for my shoes and socks, which I kept on because I was ashamed that my feet were not cloven. I couldn't find the ball and soon I started to yell, "Help! Help!"; pleadingly, "Help!"; hauntingly, "Help!" The other people in the foursome started running towards me and when they got close enough, I stepped out of the woods onto the fairway, naked, waving my wedge, and shouting, "Locusts, Locusts! Locusts!"

Indeed, the locusts were upon me, eating at my soul, driving me towards success and away from just being a carefree youth, naked in the woods, playing golf.

This is the story of my fall.

ADVICE
TO THE
BEGINNER

Golf
Equals Pain

You may hear a woman complain about being a golf widow. Big deal, it's you who is dead. It is your hands that are numb, your legs that hurt, your back that twitches, your neck that is so sunburned it's the darkest part of your body. You are the person in a terrible panic. When you play a good round, you're in fear you'll never play a good one again, and when you play a bad round you walk around the course and think, "Why couldn't I just be an ox, then I could eat this grass." You say to yourself, "What did I need this for? You know where I could have been today?" But inside you know you'll be back tomorrow, and that it's the pain that makes golf wonderful and happy.

The man who has perfected the technique of getting more pain out of golf than anyone else I know is Jack Carter. He stands up at the first tee, takes a *practice* swing and yells, "Oh! It's going to be that kind of day!" And it usually is.

If you are not the type like Jack, who constantly takes himself to task, you can always depend on your friends to do it for you. Golfers like to bug each other and frequently they say things which in any other circumstances would destroy friendships. A terrifying example of this took place one time when Milton Berle, Jan Murray, Hal March, and I were playing at the Hillcrest Country Club in Beverly Hills. (This is the only club in the world where the members get paid between $50 and $200 a month, every month, because they have oil on the property.)

First, you must understand that I love Milton Berle, I respect him and think he's a great talent, but he's a terrible golfer. He carries 18 clubs in his bag, 9 irons and 9 woods. He doesn't hit any one of them well, and he's also a bad putter. Aside from that, he's terrific. For instance, he knows how to put a tee in the ground. He taps it in neatly with a mallet.

12

On the first tee that day Milton hit a ball straight up and it landed behind him. He hit another one which went into a hedge alongside the tee and was lost. His third shot dribbled off the edge of the tee for an impossible downhill lie. Hal March bent down, picked up the little yellow wooden peg and said, "Here, Milton, don't forget your lucky tee."

Of course, even when you get off the first tee, it's no guarantee of fun and playing well can embarrass you more than if you play poorly. Before I really got the feel of the sticks, I played with one of the bosses at the Desert Inn. I shot so poorly that he said, "You shouldn't be allowed to go out and play with people. Why don't you play by yourself?" I felt very bad, and was determined not to do that again in strange company.

I was soon playing at the Beverly Club in Covington, Kentucky, and I went out with the boss, John Croft. He asked what my handicap was. Since I was a new golfer, 27 seemed about right. He gave me the shots. I parred the first hole; I parred the second hole; I parred the third hole. Never before had I parred one hole in a row. He looked at me as though I was trying to win the $2 Nassau with a lying handicap and said, "Here, Buddy, take the six dollars. You shouldn't be allowed to go out and play with people. Why don't you just go play by yourself?"

Some days you don't even have to get out and play to be hit. I was always told that golf was one of the great games to combat loneliness. If someone calls you and asks to play, it shouldn't make any difference how many you already have playing — take him along so that he won't feel lonely. If you take away enough people's loneliness, you won't feel lonely yourself. Unfortunately, there are some people who don't agree with this. One day, I called Dean Martin and said, "Dean, do you want to play golf?" And he said, "Sorry, Buddy, we already have three."

Golf equals pain.

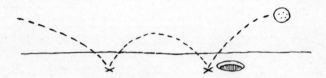

The kind of game I play – I've had a good day when I don't fall out of the cart – I could play just as well with a rock, a stick and a sweatshirt, but instead I buy the uniform – hat, shirt, sweater, slacks, shoes, socks – the works. I'm at a loss as to why I do this because everyone knows that the best attire when playing golf is socks, golf shoes, and that's it. The man who plays nude, plays happiest. But there is one disadvantage. When you are out on the course you are bound to run into the wise guy who will come over and say, "Have you got a tee?" This is the real reason you must wear something. You need a place to hold your tees. If you ever have an operation and can arrange for a small loop in your skin to be left open, you will have solved the problem, but since nudity is frowned upon by some greens committees, check with yours before you go to the trouble.

Since you will probably end up wearing clothing, make it as comfortable as possible.

Pants – The lighter the better. I suggest light-weight slacks of a synthetic fabric such as a dacron and cotton combination,

Golf Garb

flax, and nylon, preferably of parachute cloth so that at the appropriate time you can jump off a cliff and float to safety.

Shirts — There are many shirts, such as the ones that have the little alligator and the tiny penguins on them, that are made specifically for golfers.

In order to know which kind of shirt you should wear, go out and make friends with the animals. Take a trip. Go to the South Pole. See a penguin. Touch his feathers. If the mood strikes you, kiss him. Learn to love a penguin if you are going to wear a penguin shirt. Penguin shirts are regulation at Christian clubs. If you are a Jew and you want to wear one—convert.

Needless to say, the affection method cannot be used with the alligator. Alligators cannot be trusted when it comes to kissing on the lips. A pat on the tail, perhaps, but kissing, never. In order to find an alligator, you can go to the Florida Everglades, or the Bayou country of Louisiana. If all else fails, you can also call a zoo and ask for an appointment with the resident alligator.

My own shirt has an alligator on it. Once when I was golfing in Georgia I hooked the ball into the swamp. I went in after it and found an alligator wearing a shirt with a picture of a little golfer on it. He didn't even belong to a club.

If you don't own a shirt with an animal on it — you have to play a public course.

Hats — It is advisable to wear a cap when playing golf since, when you flub a shot and reach up to grab something to slam on the ground, if you don't grab a cap, you will rip out huge tufts of hair, and in an hour you'll be bald. Then someone will see a scalped human staggering around the golf course and yell, "There's Indians on the war path!" and this will bring in the Bureau of Indian Affairs, and if there's one thing you don't need in golf, it's a government bureau.

Socks – Socks are the single most misunderstood part of the golfer's equipment. Even many of the professionals who should know better recommend only a heavy wool sock. Now a heavy wool sock is a good thing to have, but not nearly as useful as a silk sock, with a very tight weave. Put the silk sock inside the wool sock and fill it with any deadly gas. Then tie a knot in it and put it in your pocket. The first time you top one, all you have to do is take a whiff of your silk socks and you'll forget all about golf and your other troubles.

Shoes – All the major shoe companies put out a golf shoe, so there are many different types on the market. Of course, that doesn't mean that necessarily you have to wear those golf shoes, and in fact, I suggest that the best way to get a golf shoe you really like is to take a street shoe that you have found comfortable for a few years, the kind you never really want to get rid of, or about which you and your wife have had the following conversation:

"How did those shoes get back in the house from the garage?"

"Well, I've been walking back and forth from the house to the garage so many years, they probably know the way by themselves and sneaked back in."

"I thought I heard some walking – did you bring them back in?"

"If you must know – yes!"

"Why?"

"They asked me to – they're old friends."

Go to a shoemaker with those old friends and tell him, "I have a friend who plays golf. I don't know anything about the game. These shoes fit him. I want these made into golf shoes." This lie will avoid a lot of trouble because the shoemaker won't ask, "What kind of game do you shoot? How do you play?" and he won't think, "Look at this guy. He's got time to go out and play golf. I'm stuck in this little shoe store all day with these nails in my mouth. I'll add a couple of bucks to his price."

You can also mumble things like: "That lucky bum that I'm giving these shoes to. He's got time to go out and play. I would have too, if it weren't for the payment that I have to come up with this week for the car." This may well get you a little help on the price and instead of $10 he'll only charge $7 for the $5 job he's about to do making old shoes into golf shoes.

That's the best kind of golf shoe to wear, not too expensive, because then when you throw them away, you won't feel so bad.

The fact is, you're still better off if you know a good surgeon who will put bone spurs into the bottom of your feet to resemble the spikes that they have in the bottom of the golf shoes.

Sweaters – An alpaca sweater is part of a golfer's ensemble. It could be 100 degrees, you still got to wear it.

Andy Williams is the guy who really popularized the alpaca sweater as part of the golfer's ensemble. You really shouldn't wear them unless you're a good golfer because they are very expensive and if you hit a ball and it goes into the woods and a twig hooks into the knit, you'll rip the sweater and there'll be $55 worth of wool laying on the fairway and all you'll have left is three buttons for ball markers.

You have to be especially careful, even if you're a good

player, of ladies with alpaca sweaters. I know a golf pro who was standing behind a lady, giving her a lesson. He was right up against her, their bodies were making contact, his arms around her arms. They were in a back swing and he looked down and noticed that the hook in his belt buckle was hooked into the back of her sweater. He didn't want to tear her sweater, so he lowered his arms slowly and while still up against her, he said, "Don't move." She looked over her shoulder and said, "All right, but I'm not going to pay for the lesson."

The garment that golfers really need is not manufactured by any big company. It is hard to come by and you will have trouble putting it on by yourself. It's called a strait jacket. Some people would say it might interfere with your swing, I say put it on, have someone bind you good and tight. Let them drip honey on your lips and allow soldier ants and bees to come around, and flies to pick and gnaw at you and bite your face, leaving bumps and torment. That's as good as playing 18 holes.

The strait jacket's the thing.

If you want to spend a swell day at the golf course you must get up bright and early. It's not good to go on the golf course late at night, unless, of course, you have a lady, a blanket, and a bottle of booze with you. Then even at night you can have a swell time at the golf course, but your score with this kind of stroking and putting is very seldom recognized by the PGA.

A Swell Day

If you arrive during daylight, it's still possible to have a swell time on a golf course. First – get to the club house and order a Ramos gin fizz. This will settle you down from the night before when you were drinking and made the date to go out to have a swell time the next day. Try very hard to give a good belch, which will take a great pressure off the sternum so that when you go into your back swing you won't feel a terrible tearing in the pit of your stomach.

Next – find your partner. Walk around the club house searchingly and, with luck, you will find out with whom you made the appointment that day. Say, "Oh, hi!" to everybody you meet. Then if somebody says, "Are you ready?" you know he's the one that has the appointment with you. Sometimes you can't tell who your partner is until you see another person running around yelling, "Hi!" Then you know he either has an appointment with you or some other drunk.

Third – follow the traditions. When you get up on the first tee, say, "I'm playing worse than my handicap, how are you playing?" Then the other person will tell a lie too, and you're ready to play.

Finally – forget about playing a good game. Remember, what counts is the deal you make on the first tee. Always let your enemy get the better of you on the first tee. Play for a small bet, no more than $2 and make sure you get the worst of it so you wind up paying from $6 to $8. This immediately puts the person you're playing with in debt to buy lunch and drinks. On a day like that, with a few drinks and a good lunch, you can come out $7 to $10 ahead.

Always remember these things and you'll have a good time on the golf course. Better yet, to hell with the PGA–go at night.

One thing that's always available on a golf course is advice. If you play like I do, you think everybody knows something you don't know. If I see a bird fly over, I think he's going to tell me something. Sometimes if he just dirties me, I'm better off.

Jimmy Durante received the best advice of anyone who ever played the game. Jimmy's first round was a total disaster. As he came to the 18th hole, his partner, who had long since lost count, estimated Jimmy's score was over 200. After holing out for 12, the Schnoz turned to his companion and asked, "What should I give the caddy?"

Without smiling, the friend answered, "Your clubs!"

Even though I know I'm having a good day if I don't lose my ball in the washer or wet myself with the water fountain, I'm not above giving a little advice myself.

For a couple of weeks I played golf every day with Gene Barry, the famous Bat Masterson of television. Gene's tall and rugged, and when he hits the ball well, it's out of sight. However, his short game is not so strong and it bothered him a bit for short, fat Hackett to beat him continually. If he wasn't doing too well, sometimes Gene would ask me for advice on what clubs to use. One day I went to the studio and got the cane he used in Bat Masterson, and waited until he had a particularly rough shot. When he turned to me and said, "What do you think I should use?" I reached into my bag and handed him his cane. "Use this," I replied, "if you make the shot now, you'll have it again on the re-run."

The best advice I ever got came under rather unusual circumstances. I was in Washington, D.C., it was late in the evening, and I was walking around and went to the Lincoln Memorial and saw the statue of the great president, Abraham

Lincoln, a man of the people. I said, "Mr. Lincoln, if you knew the trouble I was having with my golf game; I can't putt, I can't chip, I can't get off the tee, friends don't want to play with me. Mr. Lincoln, what do you suggest?"—And a voice from inside the statue said, "Go to the theater."

What I can't figure out is how he knew I was in show business.

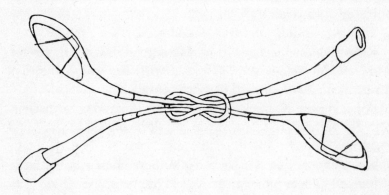

Reasons For Playing Golf

I play a lot of golf and I hate it — yes, I hate golf — but I play every day because I'm married. When you're married you're not supposed to drink and chase broads, so I play golf. I walk a lot and hit the ball and I say, "Look, see what a good time I'm having. Oh, this is swell fun." I'd like to take my swing back far as I can and hit myself in the head with that club! Why did I begin?

There are a lot of guys who start to play golf because of an unhappy marriage. You'll see a guy get up in the morning, he's had a terrible time for the past week or so with his wife over some misunderstanding. He should try to reason things out, he should try to find out what's wrong with his home and marriage, and perhaps go to a marriage counselor. But the guy goes and gets golf sticks, goes out on the front lawn, points west and tees off. Not on a golf course, just along the country's highways. He finally holes out in an Alaskan glacier.

But an unhappy marriage is not a valid reason for playing golf.

Another reason some people play golf is to exercise and lose weight. The Air Force says you burn 750 calories an hour playing golf and if you play poorly and are aggravated you burn even more than that. I should be on fire.

To really lose weight playing golf, the best place to play is in Mexico. Go to any Mexican golf course, stop at every hole and drink water. Within a week you'll have reached your desired weight. Should this not work, just place the ball in the Central Plaza of Mexico City and drive it through the front of the police station. They'll put you in the Mexican jail and you'll stay there until you reach the desired poundage.

But losing weight is not a valid reason for playing golf.

Many doctors will recommend golf to patients as a form of relaxation. After examining you for an hour or so he'll light up a cigarette and say to you, "You're too tense and anxious, get out and play golf." Likely as not he'll add, "Now, step over to this closet. I have a set of golf clubs here that I'm going to let you have for $200. Actually these clubs are worth $300 and

I'm giving you a terrific buy. They're the right size, length and weight for you to swing." If you respond that he is selling you ladies' clubs, he will probably reply, "You're going to buy these clubs or you're going to get another doctor. These clubs are prescription clubs, but I'm not writing any prescription because you're taking these."

That's another reason for playing golf—doctor's orders. This too, is not a valid reason.

Another reason to play golf is to combat boredom. As you grow older there's less and less sports activity you can do with your friends. You can't play baseball or football or soccer or hockey, but you can hit a little ball with a big stick. So you take up golf.

"What is golf?" you ask. "Just swinging a club and walking a little bit," you respond. You can even cut the walking and take a cart if you want. Sure, you start to play the game with a smile on your face, but it soon turns into a terrific pain in the heart as you find out there's more to it than just swinging the club and walking. You can walk, that's the nice part, but then you get to the part where you have to swing the club. You hook the ball, you slice the ball, and you put it straight up in the air. You take a brand new ball that costs $1.35 and swing softly once and there's a terrific cut right through the cover. You keep looking at that brand new ball — not a mark on it — just this nice cut through the cover. That's when you start getting rid of the boredom. You pick up the ball and throw it.

When you do hit a ball with the club, it slams into a tree and goes deep into the woods where you can't find it. It's never boring looking in the woods with the bears, snakes and quicksand. Best of all, you know you have succeeded in the true purpose of golf. You're no longer bored. The reason for playing golf? To turn your boredom into frustration.

When To Quit

Every man who plays golf is looking for a reason to stay off the course. I don't know why his lousy scores don't convince him. The only sure way that I know to quit is to play brilliantly. When you go out and shoot par or better every time, you'll find it's boring and it also leads to insults. Every time someone says, "What did you shoot today?" and you reply, "Even par," they are apt to quietly respond, "You're full of beans, don't hand me that crap." Now you don't want to hear that too often. Of course, you're not going to start to swing bad just because they talk that way, so par will inevitably drive you to giving up the game.

If you play well you would do far better to respond to "What did you shoot today?" with "Oh, I hardly play any more, the game got beyond me." Then they will say, "Oh, that's swell, Harry, have a drink." Golfers are so happy to see somebody goof.

There's always the chance that someone else will help you find a reason to quit. The following scene took place in the doctor's office with a friend of mine:

Doctor: Well, Buddy Hackett's friend, you're in fine condition except for two things — one is that you owe me a bill for $160. I think I ought to get paid.

H's friend: Well, Doc — I just don't have the money now.

Doctor: Listen, how do you spend your days?

H's friend: I work, and when I'm not working, oh, about five days a week I'm at the golf course.

Doctor: You're going to get good and sick playing five days a week. I suggest that you either get back to work those five days — at least until the bill is paid — or you sell your clubs at once and give me the $160 at which point I'll give you more information about the other thing that's wrong — a dark spot on your lungs.

Even a national crisis shouldn't keep you from playing golf. First of all, it's not your business. You didn't start it and you certainly can't finish it. For example, take a man who was, on occasion, deeply involved in a national crisis, the President of the United States, Dwight D. Eisenhower. A national crisis never interfered with his playing golf and golf never interfered with his running the country. He did both equally well. In fact he putted a little better than he signed bills. He was a good General, but where he learned to play golf or found the time to get down into the 80's we'll never know. I'll bet that somewhere in the Pentagon there's a putting green and a practice net and maybe a few old irons rusting away. Perhaps at one time a national crisis might be blamed for interfering with the way he handled those clubs, but golf should never be blamed because of the way he handled a national crisis.

Actually, once the great hook of golf is in you there's nothing serious enough, no possible reason why you should ever quit.

For instance, say you find yourself growing apart from your wife and children. You say, "I don't see them enough." Get them sticks – get them started in the game. Let them know what the true problems of the world are. Introduce them to what it's like to get out there and be hitting the ball straight and beautiful and then one day develop a slice that just won't quit, till the ball keeps coming back into your own golf bag. Then they'll be ready to cope with society and the pain that exists in the outer world.

Or take something as serious as a funeral, a death in the family – your wife maybe, or your pro. Now if that's not a reason to quit, there can't be any. But take a look. Where are cemeteries? In the countryside. When you drive out into the country to go to the cemetery, look around. You see green meadows,

29

woods, small ponds, and you know the reason why you *are* on earth and you think of the person just passed away and how they've gone on to the great golf course in the sky, where the worst you can take on any hole is a par, but usually you get eagles — and birdies. I look forward to a funeral as a day in the country, near the courses.

As a matter of fact, I can't wait to die.

In the Eastern section of our country there's a good part of the year when you can't play golf and you have to find a substitute sport. Some guys take up bowling. Bowling, of course, is not too great a sport, but at least it will keep you in tone and keep your back muscles working. Learn to bowl both hands. Throw the ball first with the right and then with the left. If you're right-handed, and you don't alternate like this, you will find that constantly throwing the ball with your right hand will make that arm stretch until it becomes longer than your left arm. This will ruin even a well grooved swing. If you must bowl with one arm only, make it your left. With your left arm a little longer than your right, you may improve your arc.

Skiing is nice off-season. You can have wonderful times on the ski slopes lying up to your neck in snow — it's as much fun as going out on the golf course at night. Be careful not to get your posterior frozen from the granular flakes being sifted into the ski pants. Ski pants are made out of the kind of fabric that once snow gets in, you never get it out again until it melts and wets you. Nothing feels worse than walking around with a wet crotch until it freezes and you start to click as you walk. Just be sure that you recover from all colds and fractures in time for the first day of spring.

Better than either of these, during the off-season—hibernate.

As for me, I got a practice net. A net like mine can be bought at any sporting goods store and looks something like a cage made out of mesh, with a double band of canvas folded in the back and a mat in front of the cage from which you can hit your practice shots.

It is very simple to set up the practice net. Start by sinking the four steel corner-posts into your living room floor. You'll find they're about ten feet tall to allow for the arc of your swing. Should this be taller than you are, you will have to find a method of getting to the top to hook the mesh. I suggest hiring a group like the Seven Ashtons and having them pick you up on their shoulders and seat you in the chair they use in their circus act. Then fasten the mesh to the top of the four poles, hang the fold in the back, put the covering on, and as easy as that — you are ready to start practicing.

It's very important not to have a calendar of social events while you're going to be practicing, as some guests will think you have a peculiar living room with the mesh hanging, the divot marks on the rug and the broken windows and bits of china all around. Even a golfer's wife will sometimes say, "Why is that in the living room?" You can answer, "I couldn't put it in the bedroom because we wouldn't have a place to sleep." Your thoughtfulness will be appreciated and you'll hear no more of the matter.

During the off season you may also wish to practice your putting on the carpet in your house. The best way to practice is to take a water glass and put it at one end of your carpet, and take another glass and put it at the other end of the carpet. Then take three or four balls and putt from the glass at one end to the one at the other. Do this all winter. In the spring, when you start to play again, call your local carpet store and have them redo the greens at your club so that their texture is what you're used to from practicing on your carpet. However, after doing this all winter, should you try to putt on grass, you'll find you're in terrible shape and you may wish to trade your clubs in for a vacuum cleaner.

A GAME
FOR
GENTLEMEN

Golf affects different people in different ways, but there's one way it affects all people. They become liars. Not big liars, but petty liars. Guys get a certain amount of larceny in them when they get on a golf course which they wouldn't tolerate anywhere else.

A person who wants to steal a few strokes will tell you almost anything. He'll lie about his best round, his worst round, his mother's maiden name, anything. But most of all he'll lie about his handicap. A handicap will cost you the difference between your ability and par. Golf is the only game I know in the world that you can take the best and the worst and handicap them — and the worst can beat the best. I count heavily on this.

Every guy who belongs to a golf club has his handicap listed. So when you go down to some vacation area and meet a guy on the first tee, naturally the first thing you're going to ask is, "What's your handicap?" Always be suspicious of guys who answer, "Hmmm well, my home course is a par 70"—as opposed to your course which is probably 72. Try to get him to tell you *his* course par first so you are in the position to make a few adjustments.

Guys with a handicap of 9 at their home club never end up with less than 14 on the road. To save yourself from lying the best thing for you to do is turn in accurate scores at your home club. If you do this, you'll always have a big enough handicap to take with you anywhere and you'll play a respectable game away from home.

Even just being on a golf course can affect a guy's ability to tell the truth about anything. One day I met Irving Mansfield and Phil Silvers at the Concord golf course. We played a few holes when Phil said, "Buddy, where were you yesterday?" and

I said I had worked the Sagamore on Lake George. Irving said, "Oh, I remember that, that's in Glens Falls, isn't it?" I said, "No, it's near Glens Falls, but the town is Bolton's Landing." Irving went right on, "Glens Falls, what a wonderful time I had in Glens Falls. What a beautiful village . . ."

Now everyone knows Glens Falls is a factory town with a dirty yellow river running through the middle of it, and so we knew that Irving was about to take off. "I once had the most wonderful time of my life in Glens Falls. I rented a beautiful bungalow, right on the river. There were just two of them, and who do you think I spent the most wonderful summer with that I ever spent in my life? – Greta Garbo." At this point Phil interrupted, "Irving, make it Poughkeepsie and I'll give you Merle Oberon."

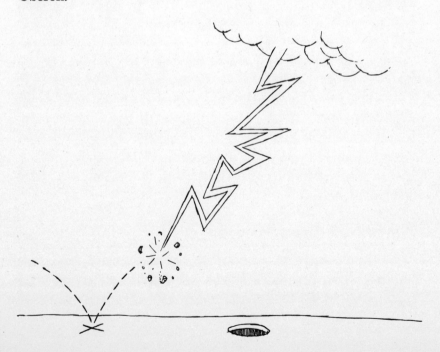

*Golf,
The Game Of
Miracles*

Based on some stories I've heard, I have begun to believe that deep down in their shafts, golf clubs are very similar to magic wands. I know that a lot of times they look like they are being used by a fairy godfather. These miracles occur most frequently when the player is alone on the course with his god, whichever one it may be. Sometimes miracles occur when playing in foursome, but even then the worshipper to whom it occurs is usually off by himself, without even a caddy around, somewhere in the rough or like Moses in a desert-sized trap.

The Penfold Case

Irving Mansfield plays a nice stick, as the saying goes, and one of the main reasons he has that reputation is because Irving has never been known to have a lost ball. No matter how deep he is in the rough, almost before he gets out of the cart you hear him cry, "Here it is!" Sometimes Irving will hit a ball into the woods, three eagle-eyed partners will look for it, and just before the five minute searching time is up, Irving will find it. The most miraculous thing happened to him once when he was playing an English Penfold. If you are familiar with the way they are wrapped, you will understand that it seemed strange to us that when he found his ball in the rough, he had hit it in such a fashion that it was back in the paper again. With that talent, he'd make one hell of a caddy.

Joey Bishop's Famous Trap Shot

I wasn't there but Joey Bishop told me this story. One time he was playing on a public course called Sportsmans — about 35 miles from the heart of Chicago. I've played there a couple of times myself, but nothing like it happened to me. On the 7th hole, Joey hit into the trap. He took his wedge and sculled the ball, it flew out of the trap, hit a tree, bounced back on the green and went into the cup. Joey didn't even say "Wow" or anything. When one of the foursome said, "What a lucky shot," Joey replied, "Don't ever say that to me – I played it that way."

"How do you play it that way? You couldn't even hit the tree again."

"Oh, no?" He took another ball, threw it down in the trap, swung at the ball, blasted it out of the trap, hit the tree again, it bounded onto the green and went right in the cup again.

Joey has never been doubted since on the golf course. He's also never made another trap shot. He hates to play any trap now that doesn't have a tree near it.

It Happened in Dayton

Once a miracle even happened to me. I was in Dayton, Ohio, during Passover week. Passover is the time when Jews celebrate the Exodus from Egypt from Pharaoh's rule when Charlton Heston led my people out of bondage, across the burning sands of the desert, through the sand traps and on to the green of Miami Beach. We celebrate this holiday by drinking wine and eating matzos – and one can improve the Holiday greatly by giving up the matzos and doubling up on the wine. You'll have a wonderful time that way.

I doubt it very much if they ever heard of matzos in Dayton, Ohio. The closest thing you could find to it is a bagel that has rolled off the truck on its way to Cincinnati.

I was in Dayton and playing golf every day at a country

club. It was a restricted country club. I didn't know it was restricted and they didn't know I was Jewish, except for one guy in the locker room who claimed he was an attendant but I think he was an inspector from the membership committee.

I went out to play with three members of the country club and we came to the third hole which had a water hazard about 125 yards out. I felt rather strong and took a 9 iron, but it wasn't enough and I landed near the edge of the water. I forgot it was Passover week and went down to the edge to see if I could hit the ball. I touched the water with my club and naturally, it parted. I walked in, played the shot, walked through, and the Egyptian caddy following me was drowned.

Playing during Passover, you got to be careful.

The Way the Ball Bounces

Of course, when miracles really do happen, it is important to know how to respond to them. At Pebble Beach golf course, Hoagy Carmichael, who is an avid golfer, teed up on a par 3 hole, picked up a club, hit the ball, it bounced once on the green, went right to the pin, and dropped in for a hole-in-one. He didn't say a word, but reached in his pocket, pulled out another ball, teed up, and said, "I think I've got the idea now."

Honesty Is The Best Policy

The most important thing about keeping score is to do it honestly. Don't try to make friends with somebody by putting down less than he really had, unless it's a lawyer or a doctor and you're looking for a little something off his bill. Don't improve your own score. Never get the reputation that the best club in your bag is your pencil. The most important reason to play the game honestly and put down every stroke you had is that otherwise, at the end of the day, you'll be short of aggravation, and golf cannot be enjoyed without a full measure of frustration and pain. If you don't take care of your score, you can be sure someone else will.

Once I was golfing with a shifty-looking stranger. After carefully counting his strokes on a particularly tough hole, I asked innocently, "What did you have on this hole?"

"Well, let me see," he replied. "It was an eight. No," he said, stopping and pretending to count them out in his head, "no, it was a seven."

"Actually, you had a nine," I was forced to say. "So I'll have to put you down for ten. You know the rules, there's a one stroke penalty for improving your lie!"

Golfers sometimes lose track of the reason for lying. They add strokes when they should be taking them off. One day I was refreshing myself at the bar when I overheard two other bums talking. One said, "I'm the worst golfer there ever was in the world."

The other guy said, "You mean next to me."

"Next to you, with you, without you — nobody is as bad as me. The grass hates me! You want to match cards?"

"Okay."

"What'd you have on the first hole?"

"On the first hole I picked up."

"Ha," replied the first bum, "you're one up."

Anyone can make a bad bet but sometimes if you use the knowledge you have of the game and people's feelings you can correct your mistake. For instance, after you hit your tee shot, and the guy hits his tee shot, don't say, "Hey, you look a lot better than you said you were." Just wait until you get down the fairway to your ball and look back at the foursome behind you. When you see someone standing there say, "How do you like this? Here I am away on a vacation and there's a guy playing behind us that I happen to know. Oh, he's a nasty guy. He'll hit right into you. He's hit at least three people I know but he keeps his insurance high and you'll get paid to forget a bad bruise from his ball."

After that always stand parallel to your opponent's head when he's playing, or even a little out in front of him where he can see you. Then, when he's about to hit, just kind of look back behind you in the direction from which the other guy's hitting and make little motions with your head like you're ducking and say things like, "Oooh, that was close." You'll get the guy pretty well shook and this will make up for the fact that he was able to outlie you on the first tee. You can't get away with it forever, but just knowing what you are trying to do will aggravate him enough so that it will work. You'll get by.

There's No Such Thing As A Bad Bet

Double Or Nothing

Phil Foster, a good friend of mine, has some very bad habits. The one that I can write about is that he will bet on anything. He will bet on throwing pebbles in a drain pipe, on pitching cards in a hat, even on his skill with a dart board that he just got for a birthday present. Once, in order to protect him from himself, I said, "Phil, I'm not going on the golf course with you any more. You always bet. You always lose and I won't be a party to it any more."

So he says, "Okay, Buddy, you're right. Let's not play for money, let's just go out and play for balls." So I went out with him. On the first tee, he makes a bet with a guy. He's only playing for golf balls so it doesn't bother me, and we play all afternoon without any pressure. Phil is playing fairly good and on the last hole he says to the guy, "What do you say? Double or Nothing?"

The guy says, "Well, I don't know whether we ought to do that." Now I'm thinking it's a good thing this guy doesn't have Phil on a usual day when he starts out with $100 and they might be playing for $600 on the 18th hole. I say to the guy, "Oh, don't worry about it, I think he can afford it."

Phil says, "Thanks, Buddy." So we played the 18th hole. As I write this, Phil is still paying off the 1,200 golf balls he lost.

Phil must be related to a man with the name of Sherlock, who's a pit boss in one of the casinos in Las Vegas. One night when Sherlock was in the pit, a guy shooting craps got so excited that his upper plate fell out of his mouth onto the dice table. Sherlock said to the stick man, "Hold the roll!"—took his own upper plate out, put it on the table and said, "The bet is faded – keep rolling, shooter!"

A Confession

Hard as it is for me to believe it now, there was one time in my life when I was playing fairly good golf. I was working in Florida and playing every day at the Diplomat Country Club, one of my favorite resorts and one of my favorite golf courses. Even the lockers in the club house, great wide things that look like storage cabinets, are the most beautiful things you ever saw.

At the Diplomat I had a friend, Jerry Volpe, from Englewood Country Club, who I had gotten a job down there working with Nick Bersan, the club professional. I was down in weight, and had no belly in front of me and between the two of them they had me playing the game pretty good. I was still holding my 15 handicap but I was shooting in the low 80's. I only played for golf balls and it didn't take long before I had the reputation of being quite a ball hustler. I would play every day, and sometimes twice a day, and each day I won between 5 or 6 balls from somebody. I never lost. Everyone had to pay tribute to play with me. And even if I played in a foursome, I wouldn't play partners. I would make each of the three guys bet me a few balls.

After I had been there about two weeks and acquired quite a few balls, my friend Joe Kellman from Chicago came into town. He asked my friends how I was doing, "Hack is hustling golf balls," they replied. "The man has almost forgotten jokes, he's forgotten friends, he's forgotten everything, and he's a golf ball hustler. It seems that he can't get enough golf balls. We must do something."

The next day Joe, Nick and Jerry took me out on the golf course. While we were playing they had some other guys load a huge paper bag with balls and put it inside the locker in such a way that when I came in with the 6 balls that I had won and went to put them in my storage compartment, I opened the door

46

and was almost balled to death by the 1,000 balls which poured out, knocked me to the ground, and left divot marks all over me.

When these balls poured all over me it made me realize my great mistake. Golf balls are a good thing to play for, but if you're going to do that, you must remember — open your locker very carefully.

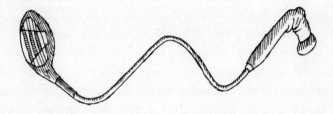

You'll find a lot of guys that have little things they do while you're putting or making a crucial shot. Some people call that gamesmanship — but it's really gromming.

There are all different types of groms and different ways guys will use them to beat you. Most sports make the people who play them better people, but golf makes them worse. When you really get to be rotten you'll be a master of the grom. As far as winning goes you'll find that you're better off to be a scratch grommer than a scratch golfer.

If you can, start your gromming before you get to the first tee. One wonderful thing to do if you're at a nice resort where they have dances is to mention little things to the guy you're playing with, like, "It must be wonderful to have a brother-in-law you're so close to."

"What do you mean?"

"You know, the guy your wife was dancing with last night."

Beware
The Grom

"That wasn't my brother-in-law," the guy will say.

And you just say, "Oh, really, ha, ha" and cough as if you're embarrassed for him.

Another thing you can do is to pick your opponent up at his house so that when you get to the first tee you can say, "I wonder why your wife was so angry. Didn't she want you to play?" This will give him a little pressure, too. If his wife came with you to the course, just kind of yell back to her as you're walking down the fairway, "I won't forget." When you yell, "I won't forget," to another guy's wife, you can be sure that he won't either.

Another good thing to say just before your opponent putts is "Who was that guy who was borrowing your car in the parking lot?" Follow it up by saying, "You know, as much as I like a guy, when he's unshaven and wearing a shirt from the night before, I hate to see him take my car. He looks like a drinker." That's good for 3 shots from less than a foot from the cup.

Phil Foster is a good example of a high handicap golfer but a par grommer. When you go into your back swing, he makes a few spitting noises. You say, "What was that?"

He says, "Ahhh, tobacco"—and he's not smoking.

One time Phil said to a guy, "Buddy Hackett and I don't play golf together any more." The guy said, "Why not?" Phil replied, "Would you like to play with a guy who coughs when you shoot, who shouts obscenities when he misses a shot, which is frequently, who steps on your ball, who walks across your line on the green, and has 17 other bad habits?"

The guy said, "No, I wouldn't."

"Well," Phil explained, "neither does Buddy."

Gleason is another one whose behavior on the golf course leaves a lot to be desired. Being raised on Chauncey Street in

Brooklyn, and most of the time in a pool room, he does naturally what others have to learn. If you take a shot, hit it up towards the pin and fly the green – somebody will say, "Too bad, the wind caught it," and another guy will say, "Gee, you hit that a little strong but it was a nice shot." Not Jackie. He'll say something like, "Nice over," indicating you flew the green with your shot on purpose and that you are really out there playing golf just to give him some entertainment.

This is small time gromming, however, compared to the guy who doesn't just want to ruin one shot but goes after your entire game. When you start in hitting that ball nice and long and straight, he says, "Boy, you could get another 15 yards outa that easily. Did you always carry your right hand on top like that? Maybe that's why you're not getting the draw out of this shot. Put it under a little more."

On your next shot, you put it under a little more and you hit the ball terribly.

"There see, you're starting to get it now."

"What do you mean – I'm only out 120 yards."

"Yeah, but you got that draw that'll give you the distance. Once you got that straightened out, you'll be terrific."

When you play with that type of grom master, within 5 holes you're going to be off the course. Better to pay him his $8 in the locker room before you go out and then not talk to him for two weeks. The alternative is to take $100 worth of lessons to correct what he helped you with.

My nomination for the world's champion grommer is a doctor who plays at the Brentwood Country Club. He never knows when he's gromming. He's just a natural born pain in the ass.

Beware the grom!

Arthur Park is a smart man who runs a talent agency in Los Angeles and belongs to the Bel Air Country Club. He had entered the club tournament in flight C, had won all his matches and was in the finals. He'd never won a trophy of any kind, and he was very excited to think that he had come this far, even in the C flight. On the first hole, Arthur and the other finalist, a real estate developer, were both on in 3. His opponent had a putt of 40 feet and Park had a 12 footer. His opponent got down on his knees behind the ball and held the putter up in perpendicular fashion to try to figure out the twists and turns of the green. Then he got up and paced off the distance of the putt, crossed to the far side of the green, held the putter up again, and took another reading. You'd think that he was surveying land to put in a housing development. Then he went around to the other side and took a look from that angle to see if there was any break. He picked up a little grass and threw it in the air. Now there are two times on the golf course when it is appropriate to throw grass. One is if you are the grounds keeper and the other is if you are playing with a hula dancer. Neither applied here, but it seemed the guy just wanted to check if the wind would have any effect on a 40 foot putt. Then he went to the far side, opposite and diagonal to the way his putt had to approach the cup to see if there was anything he hadn't noticed. At this point Arthur walked up to him with his hand out and said, "Congratulations. I concede the match. I cannot take 18 holes of this."

As I said, Arthur is a smart man who knew when he was beaten.

The only other time to concede a putt is when you already have the hole won and the other guy doesn't have a chance in the world. Then you say, "You can have the rest of that. I know you can make that one. It's yours for a seven." On the next tee, when he goes into his back swing, say, "Don't forget, I already gave you a putt." Let him think about it on the down swing.

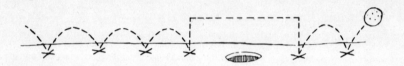

Prayer Or Swear

Golfers do strange things with the thought that it is going to improve their game. Some, for instance, pray, and unquestionably derive great benefit from it. Continual prayer on the golf course, continual repetition of the same prayer will enable any golfer, at the end of six months, to know that prayer by heart.

Even more frequent than prayer on the golf course is the lusty sound of swearing. A friend of mine was once playing golf with a clergyman. He hit the ball, hooking it into the wood, and he said, "Hell, damn!" The cleric said, "You shouldn't talk that way. God will punish you. You must learn to control yourself."

So they played a couple of more shots and my friend missed a three-foot putt and said, "Damn it! Hell! Damn!"

The clergyman said, "You mustn't do that. God will punish you if you do it."

The guy missed another shot and said, "Oh, Hell, damn!"—and a bolt of lightning came right out of the heavens and hit the clergyman and my friend heard a voice say, "Oh, Hell!"

One time at Hillcrest Country Club in Beverly Hills, George Burns was playing gin with several of his friends when suddenly someone came running in and said, "Oh, no, Mr. Schwartz just dropped dead on the 7th hole!" Burns turned a card, looked up and said, "This is a tough course."

Because of events like that, people get the wrong idea about golfers.

It's not true that they have no respect for the dead. Why once I was out in a foursome when a funeral procession went by. One of the golfers took off his cap and refused to play until the procession was out of sight.

"That was a fine thing to do," I said.

"Well," my friend replied, "it was the least I could do. Today would have been our 17th anniversary."

THE GAME
ITSELF

Ben Hogan's 5 Iron

Golf is one of the few games that is true to life. The mistakes made in life are ultimately only the fault of the person making them, and in golf too, you play by yourself. To really play you must take yourself to task for the bad shots you make and for the days that you ruin, and not blame somebody near you when something goes wrong. Just as there are bad players who blame others for their failure in the game of life, so on the golf course you may occasionally hear a player address his caddy thus, "Stand still! Don't move! You made a heel mark near the hole so I couldn't get near there . . . !"

"But sir, you were lying six anyway."

"What's one thing got to do with another? I could have gotten down in one."

"On a forty footer? It doesn't seem probable."

"All right, what is your name, caddy? I'm going to get rid of you."

Is it any wonder that caddies sometimes talk ill of their masters and that you find situations like this:

"There's a great caddy. He caddies for Ben Hogan."

"That's what I want, Ben Hogan's caddy."

Somewhere along the fairway he'll say to his caddy, "What did Hogan use here?"

"He used a 5 iron."

And Charlie Dumbtruck will take a 5 iron and end up 40 yards short and turn around and say, "I thought Hogan used a 5 iron?"

"Yes, he did. He was short, too."

Caddies can't resist their little stabs at humor, especially with a guy like Charlie Dumbtruck who's a miserable bum anyway. What better way is there for them to get even with them except to give them this information which is true but hazardous. Take, for example, the strange case of Hurwitz's 5 iron.

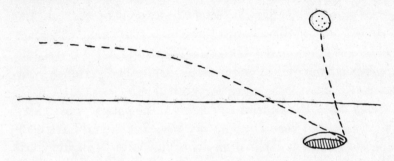

One particular day, Mr. Hurwitz was up with his caddy on the tee and said, "I think I'll hit a 5 iron."

The caddy said, "I hate to disagree with you, Mr. Hurwitz, but that shot will have to be a 3 iron. Today the wind is coming in rather strong."

Mr. Hurwitz: "I just drifted some grass and I think it's slightly cross and helping. I think a 3 iron is too much."

Caddy: "Now Mr. Hurwitz, I've been caddying on this course for many years and have noticed wind for a long time. You've only been a member two years. Hit the 3 iron."

Mr. Hurwitz took the 3 iron and creamed the shot — it flew the green, went through a plate glass window of the club house, hit his wife and killed her instantly.

A year later. . . . Same caddy, same golfer, same hole, about the same type of day. Mr. Hurwitz: "Give me my 5 iron . . . and don't tell me to hit the 3. Last time I did that I took a double bogey on this hole."

Conversations In The Twilight Zone

Then there are the caddies who are wise guys. They're always telling you stories about what other guys *did*. Or there is the caddy who can't wait to say something to the golfer who keeps trying to adjust the ball a little bit with his toe, maybe just trying to make sure it's his ball. He might inquire of his caddy: "Do you think I can get there with a 5 iron?" and the caddy will reply, "A few more kicks and I think you'll have it." Or if in passing the golfer comments, "I've never played so badly before," the same caddy will ask, "You've played before?"

Even worse than a wise-guy caddy is the patronizing caddy: "If that shot had been straight, oh, boy! You would have been on there." He knows that if *any* shot had been straight, you'd be playing golf for a living instead of suffering the way you do on a golf course.

Sometimes talking to a caddy is like a conversation in the twilight zone. I travel around a lot and play a lot of different courses. When I'm playing on a golf course I've never been on, and I can use all the information I can get, I'll ask the caddy, "What club do I need?" And he'll always say, "From here?"

"No, from Cleveland! From Des Moines, Iowa! What do you mean, from here? Of course, from here — where else would I be playing from?"

You may get even with a caddy, but you never can win. You can't punish a caddy because first of all, what are you going to do to him? Go to his boss? Who's his boss? The outdoors! He just goes to another golf course.

That same caddy will say to you, "Well, you're too much on your left foot, you're too much this, your hand should be over ... you're swinging too hard." You'll say to the caddy, "Well, how do you score?" And he'll say, "I don't know, I never played."

Sometimes caddies will do unpredictable things. There were two famous caddies at the Englewood Country Club. For all I know, one of them is still there. One of them is named Mim. Mim is a real nice guy. He works at night in a museum as a guard and during the day, because he loves the outdoors, he'll caddy. Now Mim was my caddy and Joey Bishop had a caddy named Grumpy. The reason he was named Grumpy was because he looked like the Disney dwarf. He was about 5'2" or 3". They were both in their 60's. Grumpy had blue sparkling eyes and not a tooth in his head. Grumpy liked to have a drink now and then, a little libation from which he would wind up in a Veterans' Hospital.

Once when Joey was working at the Copacabana in New York and doing a sensational job of drawing people, Jules Podell, the hurly-burly proprietor, was at the door keeping order when up comes Grumpy. Grumpy had recently been on a bender and sold the teeth that he would get every once in a while from the Veterans' Administration. He told Podell he was Joey Bishop's father and said he wanted a table. Naturally they gave him the best table in the house. He was wearing clothes he had bought at Sam's Used Clothing Store – 3 or 4 sizes too big as he liked plenty of room. He sat down at ringside, bleary-eyed, toothless. Joey came out, saw him, and went into shock. When the show was over, Jules called Joey over and said, "What's the matter, you bum, don't I pay you enough that you can buy your father some teeth?"

Some caddies, of course, are very helpful and really care. Like, you walk out and you say: "Would you like to take me out for 18?" And the caddy says, "I've already had a couple of loops today and I don't want to go any more." Therefore you don't play that day. I find this the most helpful caddy of all, the caddy who continually discourages you from playing.

Caddies are a dying breed. They are getting scarcer and scarcer while electric carts are getting more and more prevalent. Eventually, so you can drive the carts better, they're going to pave the fairways.

If you have a choice between a caddy and a cart, let the terrain of the course help you make the decision. If you're playing a flat golf course, you're better off to have a caddy; if you're playing on one that's on the edge of a cliff, you're better off to have a cart. Why? Because if you play like me, you can always take the cart and drive it off the cliff and on a flat course, you can pay the caddy to beat your head in with a niblick.

An electric cart could really help me if I could teach it how to swing so I could ride in it and it would swing and putt for me. As it is, my carts just sit there and laugh.

One advantage you lose when you play with a cart instead of a caddy is that you can't blame it for your rotten game — or can you?

A Bad-Tempered Italian

On occasion I have played with some terrible golfers, the least of which is Jerry Vale. Jerry Vale is a very fine singer of modern and traditional songs and tunes of his Italian background and whenever I play with Jerry, I always think how I would love to hear him sing an Italian song, preferably on a barge in Venice, one that's been punctured. He is probably the worst of every Italian golfer I've ever seen. I've seen some Jewish golfers that play as bad as him, but very few Italians.

Once we were playing with Pat Henry and Joe Kellman in Florida at the Presidential Country Club. Jerry kept yelling at the caddy and telling him he was in the way. He played terribly on the front nine, and must have shot close to 70. On the back nine I dismissed the caddies because I thought they were bothering Jerry and I got him a cart. Pat, Joe and I hit pretty nice shots down the fairway on 10, and we saw Jerry make 1, 2, 3, 4 shots and drive off in his cart into the rough after his ball. Now we hear him cursing the cart. By the time we're up on the green, we had lost track of him but as I got over a ball to putt, I spotted Jerry in the woods to the right. As I bent down, I heard terrible noises. I looked up and there was Jerry, trying to beat the cart insensible with a 5 iron. The cart was crying things like, "Peep...meeb...meeb...!" I was sorry I hadn't kept the caddy. He would have gone down with the first blow and Jerry wouldn't have bent the shaft of his 5 iron.

In 1954, my manager, Frank Faske, gave me a new set of Spaulding registered golf sticks. I had been playing golf for almost four years and was very skillful with my sticks. In the first three years I had learned how to carry them and get them in and out of my car trunk.

I was pretty much in love with my new golf clubs. The fact is, I planned to stay single the rest of my life, just me and my clubs — hanging out together, knowing we belong together, and having the usual fights that clubs and people have. I kept the clubs in the trunk of my car, even when I went to work at night, just in case I ran into a golf game somewhere.

One morning I got up and went down to my slot in the garage under the building. My car wasn't there. Now I thought perhaps I came home and put the car in the wrong slot and maybe the wiseguy superintendent towed my clubs away. But he hadn't seen them, so I went to the police station to report the loss of my clubs. Imagine, some damn fool stole my Cadillac just to get at those Spaulding clubs. What else could he have wanted? There were so many Cadillacs in the garage, but only one had a set of clubs like that in the trunk.

I hope the thief kept the clubs and took up golf.

The Punishment
Fits
The Crime

Greater Hate Has No Man

One day when Mickey Mantle and Don Cherry were playing, Mantle topped his ball and it went in the creek. Naturally, he took the club he was shooting with and broke it. Don asked, "What is that?" and he said, "A 3 iron." On the 11th hole Mantle hit a ball at least 200 yards out of bounds. Again he took the club he was shooting with, threw it up against a tree and bent it. Don looked at it and it was a 3 iron, and said, "I thought you broke that other 3 iron?" Mantle said, "I got 6 of 'em." "How come you got six 3 irons?" Don asked, to which Mickey replied, "Because I hate them."

Golfers do get very emotionally involved with their sticks. Doug Sanders tells about the even, smooth tempered Tommy Bolt. Tommy was about 130 yards from the green, going downwind, and he said to his caddy, "What club should I use?"

The caddy said, "Three iron."

"But it's only 130 yards and I'm goin' downwind, the pin's on the front ... Now what club do you think I should use?"

The caddy answers, "Take your choice — you have to hit either the 2 iron or the 3 iron—they're the only clubs you got left."

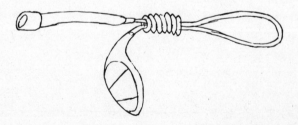

Don Cherry came close to winning the U.S. Open in 1960. He was 3 under par with 3 holes to play and 4 under was leading. Don found out that he needed to birdie one hole to tie for the lead and promptly made 7. It won't surprise you that Don has bark marks on his forehead from whacking his head against trees. He claims it's from hunting balls with his head down and running into the trees, but those who know his temper know better.

Once Don was playing in the Southwest Open in Wichita Falls, Texas. It was his home course and he started off the first round with 65, which was 7 under par and in the second round shot 70 and was leading by 4 shots. For the final 18 Don started off at the first tee with 11 golf clubs, because he broke 3 the day before shooting 70. So the first hole he hit a shot that looked like it was going on the green but it rolled off in the bunker. He threw his driver down and the shaft snapped. Now he was down to 10 and it was only the first hole. Anyway he hit it up out of the bunker about 5 feet from the pin and made the putt for a birdie. The next hole was par 5 and he hit a good tee shot, but on the fairway he took a 2 iron out and sculled it. Don thought he wasn't going to get to the green and threw the 2 iron down and it busted and he was down to 9. In the meantime the ball rolled up about 5 feet short of the hole and he made the putt on an eagle.

After 2 holes he was 3 under par but 2 clubs short of what he started with. Everything went fine till 6, a short par 3 where his 8 iron shot went clear over the green. He threw his 8 iron, it hit a tree and bent, but the ball smacked an overhanging branch on the right side of the green and dropped 2 feet away from the hole. He made a birdie there. When he finally finished the 18th hole and won the tournament by 5 shots, he had only 3 clubs left; a 3 wood, a wedge and a putter.

Being an amateur, Don couldn't win any money, but his prize was a new set of clubs.

Having three clubs left out of fourteen was just a sign of immaturity and inexperience in Don. Now he breaks every one in his bag.

Before an important shot, it is always useful to talk to your clubs. However, you should get out of the game when they start answering back. Whenever possible, use brand new clubs. Then you can honestly say, after slicing into the woods, "Gee, that's the first time I hit that club bad." Of course I only get one chance per club to say that.

There are times when it doesn't matter what stick you choose. Once I played at El Caballero, California. On the 14th hole there was a big drop off inbounds on the lefthand side. It's kind of treacherous, heavily wooded, marshy area and, of course, my ball rolled down in there. I started to go in after it when my caddy said to me, "Take a club."

"So how do I know what club to take? I can't see what the lie is."

"It doesn't matter," he said, "it's for the snakes."

Take A Club, Any Club

One time Phil Foster and Joe Kellman and myself were playing in the rain. When we teed off the starter had told us, "You can play until we get the call that the course is closed, but as soon as that happens, you'll have to come in because the carts will leave ruts."

Swinging In The Rain

Joe and I said, "Sure," but Foster just chuckled. It seemed he knew something about playing in the rain that Joe and I didn't. We went out with our carts onto the course and in a matter of five minutes, it was a muddy mess. The rain was so severe you could hardly believe it. Luckily I belong to the A.A.A. and knew I could get the cart towed in if we had to.

On the third hole, my club slipped, I fell, missed the tee shot completely and Foster said, "The secret is to keep a dry right hand. If you got a dry right hand, your club will never slip. Watch." Then he showed us that he's got a towel with him and when he makes a shot he takes the towel, puts it around his club, wraps the rest around his hand and his hand stays dry. He hit a beauty for his second shot and Joe and I were very impressed. On his third shot he again wrapped the towel around the club and his hand. He went into a nice back swing and came down in a graceful, non-slip arc. Unfortunately, the club was too strong in his hands and he drove it in behind the ball. The club stood straight up in the air, buried 3 inches in the wet ground, and because the towel was wrapped around his hand, Phil broke two of his fingers. He lay on the ground writhing in pain while the club stood right there, screaming, "My hand! My hand!" And I said to Joe, "Look, Joe, no matter what pain he's in, he's trying to keep that hand dry." At that point Foster quit.

We thought it was very unsportsmanlike and when he came out of the hospital after having pneumonia, we said to him, "Phil, don't ever start anything again that you don't intend to finish." I haven't seen him since, but I hear that he plays in a twosome with Bob Goulet.

There is very little to be said about balls as the many manufacturers conform to rigid requirements and all balls are the same size, weight, etc. The real question for a golfer is: How many balls does he need? The answer to that depends on the kind of golf course he's playing. If he's going to play a course with a lot of water hazards and no rough to speak of, he can get away with one ball and a diving suit.

There's also the problem of when to take a ball out of play because it is old. For most of us this is a phony dilemma. The greatest truth I have heard on this subject was from Sam Levenson. We were on the 16th hole at the Concord Hotel and after the tee shot there's a water hazard. Sam hooked his ball into the water, took another one, hit it into the water too, took another one out, and hit it into the water.

"Sam," I said, "why don't you use an old ball?"

"Buddy," he replied, "I never get any."

When I was a kid I carried a little Swiss knife with 25 blades. Now, to help myself out of a difficult situation, I carry some extra things in my golf bag to help the old game.

An empty beer bottle – For years I secretly practiced putting with a beer bottle and I use it on the 19th hole. If I lose a match with somebody, I always tell them I can putt, but only with a beer bottle. Having seen my regular game, they think I'm kidding, but no matter how far I'm behind I usually can get even on the putting green.

Band Aids — I never use them for myself, but if an opponent has got me stuck a little bit, I reach out a couple and say, "You need a couple for those fingers?"

"What's the matter?"

"Well, I'm sure you'll get blisters in that one spot that strange way you hold that club . . ."

"What strange way?"

"Nothing — here's the band aids. When the blister pops up, put them on."

It's good for three strokes.

Extra pencils — My opponent getting back to the golf cart, looks at the score and says, "Didn't you have a 4 on that hole? It says a 3 here."

"Well, you put the score down."

" I didn't put down a 3."

"You must be mistaken — I don't even have a pencil!"

Matches — Now the reason you carry matches is because sometimes the ball gets into deep, dry grass and you can't make your shot. You drop a lit match, walk away, the grass burns, and you play your shot. Guys will say to you, "What happened? How did that grass get on fire?"

"Why are you looking at me — am I Smokey the Bear? I don't even smoke."

A butterfly net — I carry a butterfly net because on many golf courses you see moles and gophers and I always catch gophers and take them with me to release on restricted golf courses.

A rock — This will save steps looking for a tree to slam your club against when you take a divot, chili-dip one, hit into a trap, or are just playing your usual game.

Another way to use your golf bag to better effect than just carrying clubs and balls, is to follow in the footsteps of W. C. Fields. He would secrete a dozen whiskey miniatures in the pockets of his golf bag before setting out for an afternoon on the links. "I always keep a supply of stimulants handy in case I see a snake," he liked to explain, "which I also keep handy."

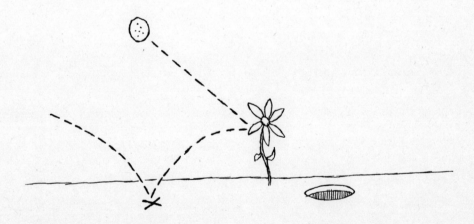

**PROS
AND
CONNING**

*A Lesson
About
Lessons*

It is almost impossible to know if your club professional can really teach you the game. The best way to find out is to ask another pro. Professional golfers always like to tell the truth about each other, no matter what they have to make up. Most pros, once they carry their PGA cards, know how to play real good, but sad experience has shown very few know how to teach. This may be because most of the time they get students like me. Once I went to a pro and it turned out that he couldn't even teach me how to drive home from the golf course. I asked him for directions and I wound up in Duluth.

I'm not the only one who has that kind of trouble. One day a friend of mine in the automobile business, who had just taken up the game, walked into the pro shop to find out about some lessons. After the pro had looked at his swing, he made the following recommendation:

"What you need is an 18 month course which would cost $400 at the start and about $100 a month after that."

"Hey," my friend replied, "that sounds almost like buying a car."

"Well," admitted the pro, "I am, but how'd you know?"

The lessons didn't do anything for my friend but at least he got to sell that pro a lemon.

There is, however, one undeniable value in lessons. They are wonderful things for the pro — to make money to feed his children, to buy his wife clothing and diamonds, and to purchase booze. If you can make friends with your pro and get some of those drinks, you must figure you came out ahead.

Of course, nobody will ever really learn how to play golf. The best thing to learn is not to play, and this can be accomplished in a minute — the minute you realize the time you waste,

the money you throw away by learning. Your financial cost can best be figured out when you realize that if you were to devote the same time and energy to business instead of golf, you could be a millionaire in approximately six weeks. Another way to calculate the true cost of playing golf is simply to subtract ten years from your life expectancy.

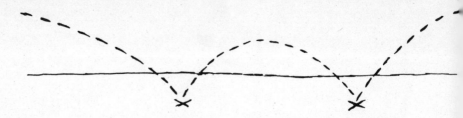

The Truth About Arnie

The reason why there are so many different types of golf equipment available is because the most important part of being a professional golfer or a club professional is the selling of equipment. Every year they call each other and discuss the situation. In a clubhouse one day I overheard Arnold Palmer talking with another pro. To the best of my recollection the conversation went something like this:

Arnold: "What do you want to swing this year?"

Another Pro: "I don't know. I feel like swinging a hammer."

Arnold: "Let's just switch clubs, and give the news out that big men need short clubs, and short men need big clubs, that heavy men need light clubs, and light men need heavy clubs, and that it's good to play with a dog team instead of a cart, that the best way to putt is with a PGA bust of Mao Tse Tung in your pocket, and that you must have a PGA Arc de Triomphe in your backyard to pitch through, and that you need a PGA approved split-level house that has a furnace that has the smell of burning golf balls."

Another Pro: "Gee, that's exactly what I was thinking."

I'd never ask a pro for advice about equipment. When I talk to Arnold Palmer we discuss dirty laundry and dry cleaning.

The pros don't know how to set up tournaments. Every day they go out to play against the best in their field and only the winner really gets paid. I wouldn't like to go out on the stage every night with guys like Bob Hope, Danny Kaye, Danny Thomas, and have only the best one get paid that night. I wouldn't like that at all. Really, they aren't working it right. They should decide in advance: "We'll all play and we'll cut it up — who the hell cares who wins?" You know, they don't give a damn about those tournaments, they just play so we can see them, that's all. They got laundries, they build golf courses all over the country, they own hock shops, clothing stores and insurance companies. If they made it up in advance, then they could drink, chase girls and do anything. Hell, I'd even help them with all that stuff.

And they shouldn't hold tournaments in a town like Las Vegas either. They do too much drinking in Vegas. One night Nicklaus was at my show and I took a drink from his glass. Now

Advice To The Pros

I know what makes him big and strong! With a drink like that, you bend down to putt and you just stay there. You never pick your head up because you are afraid to move it. Only somebody has to work your arms!

The Truth About Nicklaus

I enjoy watching Nicklaus play. I remember one hole where he didn't have a small enough club in his bag so he hit it with a teaspoon. Another time I watched Jack hit a 7 iron shot that landed on the green 14 feet in front of the pin, bounced three times, rolled and caught on the edge of the green. He had about a 42 foot downhill putt with the break going from left to right about a foot and a half. He closed his eyes, stabbed at it, it went in and he made the deuce. That was some shot — I went to the clubhouse and cried for an hour after that.

Later that day I went into the locker room and there was Nicklaus putting on a girdle. I thought at last I had found the secret of his success. I said, "Hey, Jack, since when have you been wearing a girdle?"

"Oh," he said, "since my wife found it in the glove compartment of my car."

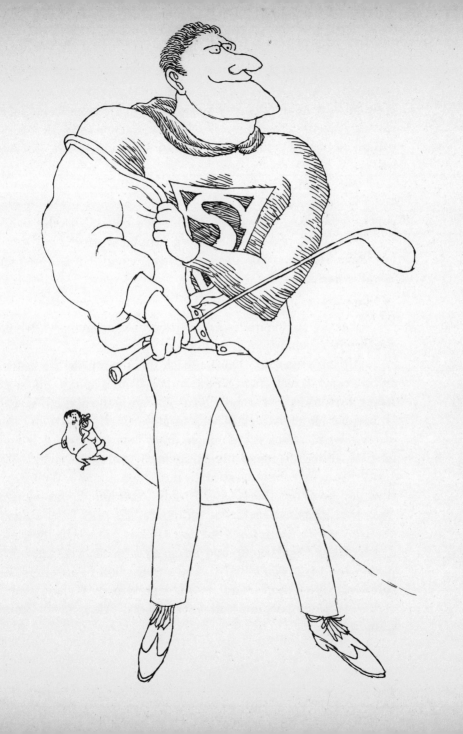

The Truth About Tommy Bolt

Doug Saunders told me this story about Tommy Bolt. Many years ago Tommy was playing in a tournament out in Texas. Now, all he needed was a little short putt to win it and he missed the shot. He went storming off into the clubhouse—all the writers behind him — and he said: "I'm not speaking to any of you writers."

"Why, Tom, why?"

"You know why," he replied. "Last week you printed in the papers — you said I was 49 years old. You know I'm only 30."

"But, Tom, that was just a typographical error!"

"Who're you trying to kid — I read it and it was a perfect 4 and a perfect 9."

Reading the Green

Don Cherry told me about the time he was playing at Pebble Beach with Tommy.

"All the greens at Pebble Beach break towards the beach, and it's hard to read them. For four days Tommy and I had been telling each other 'everything breaks towards the ocean.' We got on number eleven, which is back up towards the woods and the water doesn't affect it too much, and Tommy looks at it and says: 'I think it's going to break about 3 foot to the right,' and I said, 'Tom, it's almost a straight putt,' and he said, 'Well, ain't that the ocean out there?' and I said, 'Yeah but it's far enough away that it doesn't make any difference.' He said 'Well, I don't believe yah.' So he putts it out about 3 feet left of the hole and it runs 20 foot by the cup and never does break. Tom spins his putter and says, 'Ain't that the ocean out there? Ain't that the ocean out there?' and I said, 'Yeah,' and he said, 'Well, if it ain't gonna break the putt out that way, why don't they fill the damn thing up?' "

Beware of entering tournaments! There are some things that can happen in a tournament that you just won't believe. Robert Goulet played in the 1967 version of the Bing Crosby Tournament in Pebble Beach. He was exposed to millions of viewers all over the country. He didn't come in first — he didn't come in second. In fact, he seldom came in on any hole at all. He played so poorly that his singing teacher quit him, he was cancelled out of $160,000 worth of bookings and before he got back to the hotel at Carmel, they gave his room away to a better player. Bob spent the night outdoors practicing, caught a cold in his neck and arms and has been in traction ever since. To the day this book is written, he's still that way. In fact, Robert Goulet has never been heard of since.

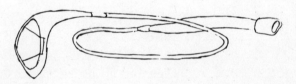

I've played in four tournaments. Years ago in Hollywood, I was in a foursome with Donald O'Connor, Tony Curtis, and the local golf pro. I don't think he was one of the great pros because he only had one foot. I didn't know what to say when the guy started to knock his ball out of the rough with his crutch because that's not really a club, and if I said, "You knocked a ball out with your crutch," and they counted it as a club, he'd be out of the tournament for having 15 clubs in his bag, which is illegal. He was Bob Goulet's teacher.

Par For The Course

The greatest thing about golf is equaling or beating par. It's a bigger challenge than getting Gleason up on a pony and few non-pros can do it. With a little luck however, even under the stress of a tournament, it can be made. Take the case of Desi Arnaz.

Desi, who's not a bad golfer, entered a tournament. On the first hole, with a large crowd lined up on both sides of the tee, he swung and knocked the ball into the gallery. It bounced off one person's forehead and hit another person in the navel. Then he played his second shot, and hit someone on the back swing. Before the first hole was over, he had struck eleven people with either ball or club. Picking his ball out of the cup he walked off the green to the clubhouse. "There's no sense in playing any more, 11 people are par for the course."

Playing Over Your Head

The tournaments in which amateurs play with professionals offer opportunities for the pros to inflict cruel and unusual punishment on their less talented friends.

Like, in a pro-am tournament, Dutch Harrison was paired with a multimillionaire who played as badly as he was rich. After one particularly rotten shot, Dutch's duffer partner's ball had landed behind a large tree, completely obscuring the shot to the green. "How would you play that?" he asked Dutch.

Dutch's classic reply was, "Under an assumed name."

Now, in 1967, I played in the Doral Open, which was sponsored by an old-time comedian named Jackie Gleason. Jackie Gleason was a terrific comedian but in his later years he started to gain weight and this took away from his humor and consequently he kind of just faded out of the picture, or I should say, fatted out of the picture. He sponsored this Doral Open and I played in a foursome with a doctor and a druggist and Bruce Crampton, the great Australian professional.

When I showed up at the golf course, I hadn't touched a stick in about 2 or 3 weeks. I was playing with a 15 or 16 handicap. In all the years and all the audiences I faced, I never was more terrified than when I was playing that round of golf, and I prayed for Divine help. The doctor and the druggist got up and they hit beautiful tee shots, and I got up and it went long and straight down the middle. I nearly fainted. Of course, Bruce Crampton got up and hit it out of sight.

We had a pretty big gallery around and at one point, I said to Bruce, "What shall I play this shot with?"

He said, "It's either a strong 7 or a weak 8."

I said, "Thanks a lot. Ask me how to tell a joke sometime and I'll tell you to do it with your mouth open or slightly closed."

I got a big laugh doing this because I was yelling to him across the fairway. Once I got a laugh from the gallery, I eased up a bit and ignored the heart in my mouth. Bruce and I had shots on almost every hole and in the first 8 holes we made 5 pars. But I knew I was playing way over my head and I couldn't go on. I had to go to the bathroom, my feet were hurting and my neck was stiff. I had a headache. I never felt such tension and such pain. I couldn't take the game any more, the pressure was just too great. It was not my business, I wasn't getting anything for it. I'm known as a comedian, I had no reason to have to fight for my life to play the game. I hated it, I hated being out there. There were a lot of pretty girls gathering around and I no longer wanted to grab my putter, I wanted to grab one of them.

The 9th hole, a par 3, was 140 yards. It's kind of an uphill shot, over some water, which, with the wind at my back, could have been done with an 8 or 9 iron. There was a big crowd on the 9th green waiting to see all the foursomes come up. I took my driver and the man on the P.A. system said, "And Buddy Hackett is hitting the driver." The crowd on the green broke like there was an avalanche. Nobody wanted to see that hit come with a driver.

No doubt I have more luck than brains, I took the driver back in a terrific swing and tried my best to miss the ball so that I'd hit it badly and top it into the water. Luckily I hit the ball where I wanted to and it rolled into the water. I went to the point of entry and took a 4 wood and trickled it out of the water, then took a 9 iron, put it about 8 feet from the pin and sank it. I had a five with two in the water. Now I was so relieved to make this 5, which was close to my usual game — 6 on a par 3 — that I got up on the 10th tee and hit 11 straight balls into the water. I was so happy, you have no idea. I started to use new balls after the 5th so I would look very sporting doing it. I only intended to hit about 4 or 5 but you kind of get into the habit when you see them balls going into the water and people are shaking their heads and nodding. "Come on, get on your stick, get on your stick," the gallery started yelling. I tried to get on my stick and fly away, but it didn't work too good.

I played the rest of the round in my own inimitable form and not counting the 11 balls I hit on the 10th hole, I think I had about 45 for the next 8 holes and it gave me a great deal of comfort.

I'll tell you this, if you're an amateur golfer, stay an amateur golfer, don't take the pain of playing in public. When you play over your head . . . you're apt to drown.

GOLF
CLUBBING

Getting
To The
Club

Be careful when you get up in the morning and say, "Isn't this marvelous! What a beautiful day! I'm going to go out there — sunshine, fresh air, green grass, the smell of wild flowers, birds chirping in the trees," because somewhere else there is a guy getting up saying, "What a beautiful day! Some lucky bum is out on the golf course in the sunshine, smelling the fresh air and wild flowers, and I have to go to work. I hope whoever he is, he slips and breaks his leg."

Be careful when you get up because you don't know if he means you or not. You might get up and go into the shower and slip and break your leg. Needless to say, this is harmful when trying to putt.

On the way to the club, dress in very somber clothes. Try to give the appearance of a Quaker or even a Minister; wear a black hat, wear a tie, get a chokey look about you. Keep your golf sticks in the trunk of the car where they can't be seen by other people, and don't ask directions how to get to the golf course. Instead, ask someone how to get to something that needs to be repaired, like: "How do I get to the so-and-so sewing machine company, my wife is sending me." That someone will pity you and won't wish for you to break your leg.

Suppose you don't heed my advice and are driving along the highway in your convertible. It's a beautiful day and the sun is beaming down. You have your golf sticks sitting in the back of the car, a nice plaid hat on; you are wearing matching yellow slacks and shirt, a brown alpaca sweater, and you hear a siren.

Now you know that police cars are never air conditioned. In fact, they're pretty warm and the uniform is apt to get sticky and even unbearably hot. Now suppose you're a policeman and you see a guy go past with his golf sticks showing. Well, that might just disturb you a little bit. I won't say that you would be dishonest enough to make trouble just because he has golf sticks in the car and matching shirt and slacks but you might want to know if those sticks were stolen. You don't have to give him a ticket. You could just talk to him for an hour and a half to see where he got his clubs or have him pull over for a minute and then make believe that you're not ready to talk to him yet. You might say, "Hold it right there," and then go on about your day and maybe come back the next Wednesday and tell him, "You can go now."

Or perhaps the officer will say, "Hmmm, that's funny—going 26 miles an hour in a 25 mile zone. What are you trying to do, kill people?"

That's the danger of wearing improper clothes to play golf. When you wear anything that looks too sharp or too exciting, you will be suspected of enjoying yourself and, to some of the people who begrudge other people fun and happiness, you will be posing a problem that they will solve unpleasantly for you. You are much better off to be somber or to just throw your clubs away and go to a Quaker meeting.

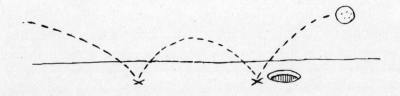

On Becoming A Member

Getting a membership in a club can be a big event in any man's life. Take Jan Murray, who has faced many audiences without nervousness, but had a few problems on his first day at the first private country club he ever joined, the Vernon Hills Country Club in Westchester. On that day the president of the club, the treasurer and one of the other big shots took him out to play. They were all pretty good golfers with handicaps of around 9 and 10. Hole after hole, Jan, who is also pretty fair with the sticks, barely hit the ball in the air. He rolled it, he ducked, he bounced it into the rough. It was just terrible, and he got more nervous and more nervous thinking of these three guys saying to themselves, "My God, what did we take in as a member here?" Jan kept apologizing, saying, "Really, I don't play this bad. You know, I really play much better."

After five holes of acute misery they teed off on the sixth hole, a short par 3, heavily wooded on the sides. Jan sliced the ball into the woods. Never had he felt so humiliated, so embarrassed, so in need of a friend, and his caddy, who had never spoken to him on the other five holes, gave him a real sour look in the eye. Finally Jan found the ball and stood there looking at it. He turned to the caddy and said, "Have I got a shot to the green?" Very wryly he replied, "Mr. Murray, I'd say you have several shots to the green."

Even at that, Jan was better off than Jack Carter.

Jack has tried to join many different golf clubs. Usually a friend who is already a member brings him up for membership, but by the time the committee meets, the friend is the first one to vote against him. There are even a few guys who lost their own membership merely because they had Jack out as a guest.

I belong to a club in Los Angeles – The Brentwood Country Club. That's a Jewish Country Club. In Los Angeles, the country clubs are either Jewish or Gentile: Lakeside – Christian; El Caballero – Jewish; Hillcrest – Jewish; Los Angeles Country Club – Christian. The Bel Air Country Club is a Christian club. If you are Jewish and you have clubs you can play there but you can't be a member. In fact, Eddie Fisher and I played at the Bel Air Country Club with Pat Boone and Andy Williams and it rained on me and Eddie. I don't know how they worked that but the next day we took them to lunch at the Brentwood Club and they got heartburn.

This Jewish club, Gentile club situation can cause real problems.

James Garner is a fantastic golfer, about a two or three handicap, and a regular gentile. He's married to a Jewish girl, and because he's married to a Jew, none of the gentile clubs will take him in as a member. Because he's gentile, none of the Jewish clubs will take him in as a member. Consequently, he can't belong to any club. You can see him at five and six o'clock in the morning, standing on Wilshire Boulevard driving balls into the traffic. It's a menace not having him as a member of a club somewhere.

The Bel Air Country Club, which wouldn't take in James Garner, was willing to take Jack Lemmon although Jack Lemmon is also married to a Jewish girl. However, his wife said things to him like, "Go ahead, Jack, you join Bel Air. I'll wait for you in the parking lot. The children and I can watch you play golf through the fence. We don't mind that. You can go to the dances, too. I'll sit outside on the curb until you're through."

Jack is now a member of the Brentwood Country Club. Since he has broken the barrier, I'm sure that Brentwood will now take in more Christians. I'll even nominate them, as long as they keep playing as badly and betting as much as Jack does.

Hillcrest was the first Jewish club built in Los Angeles. When a few local Jews found out they couldn't get into the Christian clubs, they bought land and started to build. They said, "We're going to take in everybody." They were going to show everyone how magnanimous they were, but they struck oil and then they said, "To hell with them. Just Jews here, that's all; just Jews." There's a rumor that the Brentwood Club may take in Christians, but they're still checking for oil.

All clubs should be like the one I belong to in New Jersey. The reason I joined the Englewood Country Club was because they didn't put any restrictions on the membership. There they have Jews, they have Christians, they have Negroes, they have Puerto Ricans, they have Japanese — they have such fights, you wouldn't believe! You have to walk through blood to get to your ball.

The real reason so many guys want to be members of a golf club is because it's supposed to be good for business. No doubt many important deals are made on the golf course, because if a guy's a golfer, you get the feeling that he's probably sporting about

The Golf Biz

things in general and it's more of a pleasure to make a deal with a guy like that and even have him cheat you a little than to make one with an unsporting guy who gives you an even count in the office.

There's a story that illustrates this point. One day there was a real estate salesman playing at the Brentwood Country Club, who for days and days had been trying to interest a financier in a big deal that he was putting together. The salesman was scrupulously honest and cared so much about the game of golf that he wasn't even throwing the match.

When they finished the front 9, the salesman was still pitching both balls and property. Finally it looked like he had the deal wrapped up and they went up to the 10th tee for everybody to hit off, but when they got down on the fairway to look for the balls, the salesman couldn't find his. He looked and looked, but still he couldn't find it. Finally he glanced at his hand and saw that he was holding his club, his tee and his ball. In the excitement of almost completing the deal he had simply forgotten to tee off. He didn't want to walk back to the tee because he thought that the financier would think that he was such an imbecile that he couldn't possibly know about a good piece of land to sell, so he took his ball and tossed it into the rough. He gave himself the worst of it, a really bad lie. However, the financier saw him toss the ball, walked up to him and said, "If you would cheat me for a lousy $2 Nassau by trying to put a ball in play after you lost your tee shot, do you really think that I would dare go into business with someone like you?" and he walked off the course.

Or take the case of Joe Kellman. One of the saddest sights in the world is to watch Joe, who owns a glass company in Chi-

cago, play golf. Joe is a fine golfer and consistently shoots in the mid 70's. Because there's a lot of business done through insurance brokers who recommend to clients where to buy their replacement glass, Joe frequently takes brokers out to play. Most of these guys have no more right to play in his league than I have to hunt the Kodiak bear with a zip gun. Joe has played with the worst cripples imaginable. He plays with guys who are four feet tall and have a five foot club; he plays with long skinny guys who come out with their wives' clubs or with something that they borrowed from a kid somewhere, maybe toy clubs by Mattel. These guys say to him, "Did you see my ball, did you see my ball, did you see my ball?" and Joe, with a smile on his face, will say, "That wasn't a bad shot. Here, it's right over here, behind the tree under the rock. Another two or three like that and you will be off this tee."

I don't know how much longer he can take it. Right now Joe may be sitting at home planning how to burn down his glass business. Either he gets rid of his business or his clubs. He can't keep them both because no matter how good golf is for his business, his business is no good for his golf.

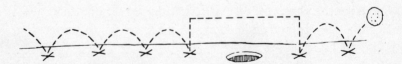

For years the Desert Inn has been one of the outstanding hotels in Las Vegas, and one of the most successful business ventures of all time. In the week or ten days prior to the 1967 Desert Classic Tournament, which was to be conducted on its first-class course, a great many rooms in the hotel were occupied by Howard Hughes, financier, munitions magnate, motion picture producer, paint manufacturer and a man whose life story in one form or another has made a fortune for people other than himself. He had a lot of rooms, in fact he had one room just for sneakers. Now the hotel notified him that he would have to give up his rooms because they were previously booked for the golf tournament. It is well known that nobody tells Mr. Hughes where to go, and so he became indignant, to say the very least, and said straight out that he wouldn't give them up. The head of the Desert Inn organization, Mr. Moe Dalitz, who is quite a big wheel in his own right, went to see him and said, "Mr. Hughes, you've been a guest here for many years and we all have a great feeling for you, but we need those rooms." Mr. Hughes replied, "How much do you want for the hotel?" and Moe Dalitz said, "$13,000,000!" He said it with a smile on his face because he knew the hotel was only worth $11,000,000. Now Howard Hughes had just received a check for $625,000,000 for selling his stock in TWA and he said, "It's a deal, now don't bother me, it's now my hotel. Here, bring me change," and handed Moe the check for $625,000,000 and Mr. Dalitz said, "We don't have the change right now, so we'll have to change the odds for an hour."

The next day Mr. Hughes was in command of the hotel and of the offending golf course as well, but until he had his name on the gambling license and the liquor licenses, it wasn't quite his. So he called the Governor, Paul Laxault, and he called the town commissioners and he called several other people and he said, "I want to build a $6,000,000 hospital complex for the city of Las Vegas and area." Surprisingly, it still took a few hours before he had his license approved. Now he had $19,000,000 invested and to this day I don't think he has gotten even, although they might have changed the odds a little bit.

The PGA had been working on the Desert Inn course for a year to get it in shape, elevating traps, redoing greens and the like. Mr. Hughes heard from them a couple of days later. They said, "We want to check out the course," and he said, "I don't want you here," and with a flick of his tongue moved the whole tournament to the Stardust Hotel's golf course. I have a feeling if he doesn't like the way they run it there, he'll turn that course into a corn field.

Glub Gleason

The exact opposite of Mr. Hughes, although he's almost as rich, is Jackie Gleason, the second funniest man in the world. He will turn a corn field into a golf course. Gleason is a serious golfer and plays almost every day of his life.

Jackie is somewhat plumpish and the worst thing that anybody who works at the course where Jackie plays can hear, is the fact that he has decided to lose weight. When he decides that, he increases his number of rounds every day. Jackie has a golf cart that's as fast as a slow sports car. He'll get into his golf cart, rev it up pretty good, and then say to his caddy, "We got to play a lot of golf, because I got to get rid of some weight." Jackie has no regard for the greens, tees, anything. He drives his cart right up onto the tee where there's a big sign that says, "No carts allowed." He stops and parks on that sign. Then he sits in the cart, the caddy bends over, tees up the ball, Gleason gets up, walks one step, swings, hits the ball, the cart, the caddy — in one shot (and a very nicely executed shot) at the same time and tells the caddy, "You were in the way, pal." Then he gets back in the cart and starts racing towards where his ball went and the caddy has to go full tilt to get there first to improve the lie. The last caddy that he had gave up golf to represent the United States in long distance running. Gleason starts off with a caddy who weighs 180 pounds. When the caddy is down to 131, Jackie goes off the diet.

There's nobody who cares more for the game than Gleason does. He's turned a sport into a religion. Jackie Gleason has his television show coming out of Miami Beach, Florida, for only one reason — he loves golf. A few years ago he left New York and moved to Florida to the country club where he decided to play out his life on the course. When CBS begged him to go on television again, he said, "There is no way to get me on television unless you move CBS down here." Consequently, CBS built the facilities necessary to do an entire show out of the Convention Hall in Miami Beach.

After a while, Jackie decided the local country club was no longer private enough for him and he got involved in the

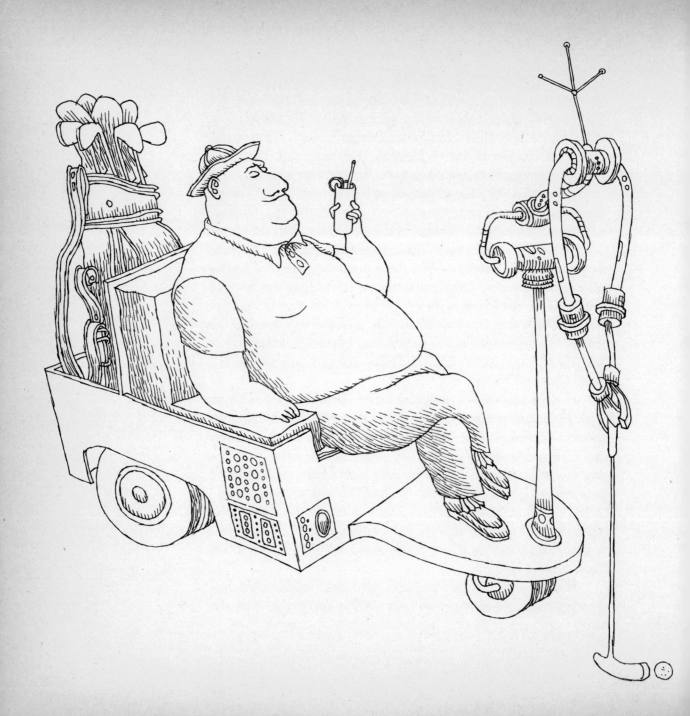

Country Club of Miami, which at present has about 170 members. On the grounds of the Country Club of Miami, Gleason caused to be erected an entire rehearsal hall, and a building that could house U.S. Steel, DuPont, General Motors, or any other large firm. He just calls it —"Gleason's Headquarters." It is very seldom that anybody is in it except for a few receptionists who say, "He's out on the golf course now." He also built a home that has a 200 foot frontage on the course. Part of it is Jackie's pool room, which is a building where he has his own pool table, billiard table, a tremendous bar and holes sunk right in the carpet with real golf cups so he can keep in practice. He has a large selection of clubs and putters for guests and he can beat you at any one of them.

Knowing this I practiced for a few months with a beer bottle and then I went down to see him. I said, "Jackie, how good do you putt?" "Mmmmm, I'll take you on, pal." But I beat him with the beer bottle. The next time I came back, he beat me because there is more beer in him than I could ever get in me.

Let Gleason be a lesson to others who profess a love for the game. Don't think yourself a serious golfer unless you are ready to move your entire business to where the golf is and not just leave your business occasionally to go play golf.

Glub Goulash

In 1963 Nicholas Reisini was lying in bed in a hospital. There was nothing wrong with him except that he wanted to make a deal with me to go make a movie behind the Iron Curtain. He called me to come over, figuring, "How can you holler for a lot of money when a guy is lying in a hospital bed?" I told my wife, Sherry, "We are now going to go see a man in a hospital who claims his legs are broken from a fall in a hotel somewhere, but there is nothing wrong with this man, and I know it. At one point in the conversation he's going to say to me, 'Me, lying in a hospital bed like this, and you take advantage of me?'" So we went to the hospital and he says, "I have a story, and it's so beautiful. It's about a little girl who leaves London and goes with her mother and father to Budapest and she spends the summer there. It's a beautiful story. There is a crook named Kovach and this crook is kind of a nice crook."

"Can I see the script?"

"You'll see the script when you get there."

"In other words, you don't have a script."

"How could you talk to me like this, when I'm lying in a hospital bed?"

"We didn't even get to the money yet, and you said your best line."

"Look, don't you want to take your family to Europe, all expenses paid?"

"Yeah, we're going to do that. We're saving up for it. That's why we want to get all the money we can now, so we can save up for it."

"We'll pay all your expenses."

"I'm going to be working. When am I going to get to see anything if I'm going to be working?"

Finally we arrived at a deal and I left for Budapest. I was there for quite a few weeks and we didn't have one foot of film. I was going insane trying to find things to do; I didn't know how to speak the language, I couldn't get the food I wanted, there was no way of translating unless you called the porter who spoke English, and you could never find him. You sat down in a restaurant and they just gave you what they wanted. Once for breakfast they gave me a wet rag — things like that.

Naturally, I kept asking them where the golf course was and they keep looking at me like I want to start another uprising.

Finally I made friends with a guy named Dave Betz who was with our legation, that's the American Legation in Budapest. When I say "our," I don't want you to think there was a special representative from my temple. Dave Betz and I became friends and I kept rushing to him with any problem I had — one of which was that we didn't know how to get hamburgers for my kids. He invited us to his house and his wife, Dorothy, gave my kids some hamburgers. I felt funny being a big movie star in Europe making a picture and "schnorring" hamburgers.

I told Dave how I loved to play golf and he told me they had built a 5 hole golf course on Legation property up on the side of a hill. They had 5 par-three holes, and the longest hole was about 165 yards. The guy who ran it was a full Colonel named Fred Roberts who was the Air Attache for the United States in Hungary. Now Fred Roberts is a man about 5′6″. He has very powerful hands. I think he would get up early every morning and run through the woods squeezing trees. He'd squeeze 'em, stopping the circulation of sap, and the upper branches would wither, leaves would drop and then he'd let go.

I think every tree in Hungary had a circle around it from his hands.

Fred told me how they had carved this golf course out and how the Hungarians who were watching them build it and who were working for them too, had no idea what they were doing. Everyone was sure that it was some kind of missile installation that was going up, especially as our Air Attache didn't even have a balloon. Personally, I think he was there for a lot of golf and a little spying.

I went out and played golf with him. I had better soil in my cuff than they had at that club. What they did have though were a lot of strange rules. For example, you were penalized two strokes for balls hit into Communist territory. If you got up on the tee and you went in front of the markers, your opponent was permitted to throw pepper in your eyes. There were goulash hazards, noodle traps and other things you don't frequently see.

When I left the course on the side of the mountain, having made a few mistakes, I was the most thoroughly seasoned golfer. I mean I was seasoned – covered with paprika, feketaborsch, which is black pepper, and little pieces of carp were stuck in my ears. On the whole, I didn't look too good and I think it was the worst slant of golf that I ever played.

The Last 18

A friend of mine died and found himself applying for membership in the great country club in the sky. The committee looked at his dossier and sent St. Peter to discuss one failing with him. "You lived an exemplary life," St. Peter began, "but there is one very large black mark on your record. It is written that you once took the Lord's name in vain while engaged in the honorable game of golf. You know, I play a bit myself and I understand how frustrating the game can be. If the circumstances are extenuating, perhaps we'll be able to overlook your error and let you in anyway."

"Well," my friend explained, "it all happened just last year at our club tournament. On the final day I had it won coming to the 18th hole. All I needed was an easy par four to be club champion. My tee shot was beautiful, 230 yards right down the middle. However, when we reached the ball it had landed right at the base of a small sharp rise in the fairway and there was apparently no way to blast over it in the direction of the pin."

"And that was why you took the Lord's name in vain?" asked St. Peter.

"Oh, no," my friend continued. "I was distressed, but I knew that if I used the right iron and hit the ball just right, I might still leave myself in a position to get that par. Carefully, I selected my club, slowly I brought it back and with a perfect swing I knocked it straight towards the green. To my amazement, it took a crazy bounce on the edge of the green and rolled backward into the trap. When I got there only a tiny part of the ball was visible in the sand."

"Oh," St. Peter said, "something like that once happened to me and I can certainly understand how this could upset you.

That is why, I assume, you took the Lord's name in vain." With that St. Peter looked as if he were ready to unlock the gates and let my friend in.

"Oh, no," he replied. "I was disappointed, but I screwed up my courage and took my wedge, carefully checked all the details of the shot and hit just the right distance behind the ball. I was perfect and the ball stopped less than a foot away from the cup."

St. Peter looked incredulous, "Good Lord, don't tell me you missed the Goddamn putt!"

He got in.

The Responsible Club Member

Whether you are playing on your own course or not, treat every golf course like it's your own property. Try your best to keep it in good repair, replace all divots, tee up only where the markers are, fix all ball marks on the green, drive carts only in the rough, and never drive a cart on the fairway in wet weather. Treat the property like it's your own, and if you can, sell it!

GOLF, BOOZE, AND BROADS

Years ago, when I was a young man, I was a wild nut and traveled with the booze 'n broad set. All we cared about was drinking booze and chasing broads. I didn't care if I ever caught them, it's just the thrill of the chase. Once I caught one and she said, "What do you want?" I said, "I don't know, I never caught anybody before."

Those days are gone now. Now the only thing that I'm interested in is playing golf. Truthfully, I shouldn't write that. I'm still interested in booze 'n broads but it's frowned upon when a guy's married for him to be drinking and chasing, unless it's done within the confines of his own home where, unfortunately, there's seldom much of a selection. Therefore, it behooves us guys who are traveling around to find other interests to use up the energy that is stored within. Some guys decide to bowl, some guys will ride horses. I picked golf, and I play golf and walk every day, swing at the ball, keep my head perfectly still, bring my arms back in a nice smooth arc, all the while mumbling, "This is better than booze 'n broads." I always mumble it. If I said it clearly, they'd put me away in a rubber room. But there are a lot of guys who believe that golf is the answer to everything.

Take Jan Murray, take like Phil Foster, or take a guy like Joey Bishop. They swear that golf is better than booze 'n broads. They tell me, "You'll love golf — wait till you make a few pars every day, you'll see how good you feel." I tell them, "You make one broad, you feel good for a year." I don't mind playing, but I don't want to be talked into how much I love it.

Anyway I really wanted to find out if golf was better than booze 'n broads, so I went to Jimmy Demaret, one of the greatest names in golf. I said, "Jim, the truth. Is golf better than booze 'n broads?" Jimmy looked at me with a big smile on his face and said, "I don't know about you, young fellow, but I've been playing golf man and boy for thirty-four years — to get money for booze 'n broads."

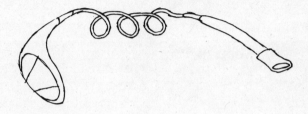

I got married on account of golf.

In 1950-54 I lived at the Concord Hotel in the Catskills, and if you know anything at all about resort hotels, you know there's check-out day and check-in day, and that day is Sunday. Sunday nights I'd always look around to see who the new check-ins were and find a new girl friend for the week. I would find a girl, by midnight profess my great love for her, and be with her every moment I could when I wasn't playing golf. Every evening I would be with her, and we would dance, and frolic and laugh.

Come Friday night and my true love would show up — Jimmy Demaret. Jimmy had a wonderful apartment on top of the club house, and on Friday nights we would gather up there, all the guys who were the afficionados of golf, all the guys who really adored golf professionals, and guys who came along with Jimmy just to listen to the wisdom that dropped from his mouth.

Friday nights we'd go up there, and among other things, talk about the different ways to make martinis. He told me about

Jimmy's Place

113

a guy who had vermouth in an atomizer. In fact I learned more about how to make those shots than any other. But most of all we told golf stories and talked golf. They were the most wonderful sessions in the world. I'd sit there with my tongue hanging out, eyes popping out of my head listening, wanting to emulate this man in every way.

I can't tell you how much I looked forward to these Friday night things. Friday night would come up, I would go to Demaret's apartment for the golf session, the phone would ring, and a girl would say, "This is Alice, or Greta, or whoever, where are you?" And I would say, "I'm with Mr. Demaret . . . and I am listening to golf."

"Well, when will I see you?"

"When Mr. Demaret leaves."

"I'm going home Sunday."

"Well, I hope you don't leave until after he does because then there is very little chance that I will see you at all."

"What do you mean? Who am I going to have dinner with?"

"Why don't you have dinner with the waiter as he is always very close to the food?"

"You mean I won't see you this evening?"

"I doubt it very much."

"Can't I come up there?"

"Hardly, your handicap is not low enough."

"What happened to all those things you said?"

"I said them, and they were all true, but now there is golf to be spoken about, and golf to be enjoyed, and you must forgive me. Adios." And I would not see the girl any more.

Then one Friday Jimmy didn't show up and I got married.

Dr. Hackett's Diagnosis

When I was a kid I used to carry the game bag of a guy named Ash Resnick who was a super basketball player for the original Celtics. Ash was about 6'3", weighed 235 lbs., and was one of the world's strongest human beings. Ash never smoked, never drank, never ran after skirts, and he hit a golf ball like a little girl. Come to think of it, he's the only guy I ever knew who tried to play golf that didn't smoke, drink whiskey and chase. It's a good thing I'm writing this book or I'd have never figured out what was wrong with Ash's golf game.

First Things First

Don Cherry, a great golfer and a fine singer, was engaged to Joy Blaine, one of the dancers in the show at the Sands Hotel in Las Vegas. On the day before his marriage, Don was playing with Bo Wininger, Joey Bishop and Tony Fabrille, at the Desert Inn Country Club. Don was just about to tee off when Joy showed up in her bridal outfit. Don turned around, looked at her and said, "Joy, I told you only if it rains!"

(It's not generally known, but Eve was born on a Tuesday and Adam said to her, "I don't know who you are, and I guess I'm going to marry you and you will be my wife, but remember, Thursday is my regular game.")

Don and Adam did it right. Those couples never had another argument about golf. My story, however, is a sad one. Late in

the afternoon of my wedding I was wearing tuxedo pants and was about to put the studs in my shirt when Alan King called and said, "Let's play a few holes." I said, "I'm getting married."

He said, "If you're going to allow anything to interfere with your golf, give up one or the other. Either give up your clubs or don't go through with the marriage."

I understood the wisdom of his remark and I also knew he had been married for a long time. We played the first hole of the International Course at the Concord. I had a bogie, and Alan had a par. I got up on the second hole and hit into the woods. I took a second ball and did the same thing. Alan looked at me and said, "I don't think you should get married. Any man who loses his swing at the thought that he's getting married in half an hour, has very little chance of swinging well after the ceremony." I told him that it had nothing to do with the impending marriage, it was just that before coming out I had talked to my wife-to-be, and it sounded like I was talking to a stranger. "Is that what's bothering you?" he asked. "Let me tell you that I've been married 8 years and every day it sounds like I'm talking to a stranger. It happens to everybody."

I hit the next ball about 260 down the middle and shot an even 40 for that nine. With this kind of golf under my belt I knew that marriage could be a good influence on the game and was very happy to go through with it.

That night, after the wedding, we left for Bermuda and stayed at the Coral Island Club. Jerry Volpe, the Englewood golf pro, knew where we were going on the honeymoon and he went to stay at a beach club with a big golf course nearby. The next day he showed up at the Coral Island Club. He knocked on our door and I opened it. Without saying a word he handed me something. I looked at it and yelled, "Oh, boy! My driver!"

My wife looked at me and figured that if this man is this happy over his driver on the honeymoon, married life will not be too sweet in the future. From that day on she took a terrible hate to golf. Since then I've bought her all kinds of clubs and tried to introduce her to people that play, but I've never succeeded in compensating for that day that I obviously preferred the company of my driver to my wife. With my great love for the game, I should have married a golf ball.

An avid golfer, seeing a beautiful, beautiful girl, fell madly in love with her. He forgot all about golf. Their courtship took all of his time and he couldn't rest until she promised to be his. Finally they were married, had a magnificent honeymoon, and returned. Soon after he said to her, "Honey, you know I love golf and though I don't love it nearly as much as I love you, I haven't played since we first met. I want to play today. I'll be back in a couple of hours."

She said, "Why don't you take me along, I love to play golf."

Joyously he said, "Are you a golfer? I never even asked. What's your handicap?"

She said, "Eleven."

The Story Of A Happy Marriage

He said, "Eleven? That's my handicap — eleven." And they went out to play. On the first tee he said, "Wait, I'll hit and then you can go up to the lady's tee."

She said, "I play from the men's tees."

The first day she beat him two up. They went out and played again the next day and she beat him three up. They played the third day and came to a five par hole and from the men's tee, she was on the green in two, about 40 feet from the cup. She said, "Oh, I'm so excited! I've never been on a par-five in two before. If I sink this putt, it'll be my first eagle! I'll kill myself!"

Her husband said, "It's a gimmie."

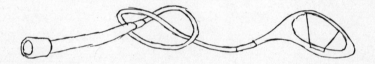

Sherry

My wife, Sherry, is a dancer and though she certainly has a natural rhythm, she's not a particularly strong girl. After we had been married a while I thought that since I enjoyed her company at home so much I would also like to have her with me on the golf course, and so I sent her out to take some lessons. The right clothes, carefully matched clubs, dozens of balls and the lessons were pretty expensive but I didn't mind it as long as they were going to be used. And they were used — against me.

When she was ready we went out together. We got on the first tee and I watched her get over on the ball and potchgee around. She teed the ball up, she walked behind it, carefully bending down – she looked terrific dressed all in white. She had on a little white cap, a white top, white shorts and white shoes and socks. I looked at her and began to wonder how she was going to swing her arms since she's built rather robustly and very feminine. Finally she went into a back swing and took a nice, smooth, soft swing and hit the drive a little bit off the toe of her club about 45 yards, including a good roll.

I tried to explain to her she should face a little more to the left because she's hitting the ball to the right. She said, "It doesn't make any difference if I hit it down the right side as long as the person I'm playing with hits it down the left." I said, "Where did you hear that?"

She said, "Well, when Lorraine and I went out to play, the caddy said it didn't make any difference, because we could always change balls. If I'm on the right and she's on the left, her caddy and my caddy tell us to switch balls and keep playing." So I discovered how those friendly caddies made life easier for themselves when they took out women.

By the third hole she discovered that I didn't hit the ball the way her golf pro was telling her to. As I recall, on the 18th hole, after she told me all she learned in her lessons, I went into a back swing, took a nice smooth swing and hit a drive a little bit off the toe of my club about 45 yards, including a good roll.

I have since canceled her lessons. Also, our outings together on the golf course. In fact, I think the last time I saw her was in 1959.

*Advice
From
The Wife*

One night Don Cherry was one of my dinner guests. Don at one time was married to Miss America, Sharon Kay Ritchie. Don Cherry is now married to a girl named Joy Blaine. Before they were married they were all friends with each other. Don Cherry and Sharon had two children, therefore Don would often come to Sharon's house to visit his children. On this particular night Wm. B. Williams and his wife picked up Sharon and Don and, although they were no longer married, brought them together to my house. In the course of the evening, we all started telling stories, and Sharon told about the time Don played at the Master's and how helpful she tried to be during their first year of marriage. Don was paired with Ben Hogan and shooting rather well, except for the 15th hole, where 2 days in a row he hit his second shot in the water. The third day on the 15th he hit an enormous tee shot and was way out in front of the field. He knew he might get on in two and possibly eagle the hole which would put him right back in contention. Sharon was in the gallery and, remembering he had put the ball in the water for two previous days, was quite concerned and wanted to help him. She walked over to tell him that he could use enough stick, or "piece of stick" as she put it, as she was not too well schooled in the game. At this point Don interrupted and said, "No, no, that isn't what you said at all. You came over to me and you said, very plain, 'Careful, honey, remember what you did the last two days,' and Pow, I dumped it right in the middle of the water."

Now she's married to Kyle Rote.

If your wife plays golf, inevitably the day will come when you decide to play a mixed foursome — you and your wife play with your best friend and his wife. Unless everybody is really good and able to keep up with each other, allowing for the handicaps and for the women teeing off ahead of the men, at the end of three holes there will be very little left of two marriages and four friendships. There will be nothing at all in the way of friendship between you and the other guy and for sure his wife and yours won't be speaking. He will probably try to run your wife down with the cart and you will now hate his wife while for years you thought she was kind of a cute dish. Oh, maybe you'll still have a little yen left but that's all. I don't suggest mixed foursomes. I don't even suggest it for dancing.

A Mixed Twosome

This is something that is really difficult to write about since everybody's approach to both subjects is entirely different. Still I'm sure that anyone who has ever played golf and anyone who has ever tried sex will find the parallel between the two. The objective is the same: to be as close to par as possible, to execute the proper shot and get the satisfaction of a job well done.

Although they are so similar in thought and in motivating force, you will find that one is very detrimental to the other. As highly as we may think of a partner, either in golf or in sex, the chances are we would not care to have that partner join us in both. Seldom in my youth, when I began to play golf, would I get up in the morning and turn to my companion and say, "That was great, baby, now let's get to the tee." I found that the people who I selected to join me in my boudoir would ofttimes have various encumbrances that would inhibit their swing. In fact the more their swing would be inhibited by their encumbrances, the more I appreciated them. If you allow such a playmate to become too deeply involved in your life, eventually she will say, "Why can't you take me to the golf course?" And when you take her out there and you try to teach her and discover how inept she is at the game, you will lose your pleasurable feelings about her in other areas. Keep these things separated, but don't overdo one in favor of the other for finding that you excel in one or the other and spending more time on the green or in the bedroom will eventually affect what you're trying to do in both.

However, if you must pick between one or the other, I think you're better off to staaayyy . . . wittthhhh . . . that question will be answered in my next book.